Norse Mythology

Norse Myths from the Birth of the Cosmos and the Ice Giants to the Appearance of the Gods and Ragnarok. Conspiracies, Evil Gods, Mythological Monsters and Legendary Heroes.

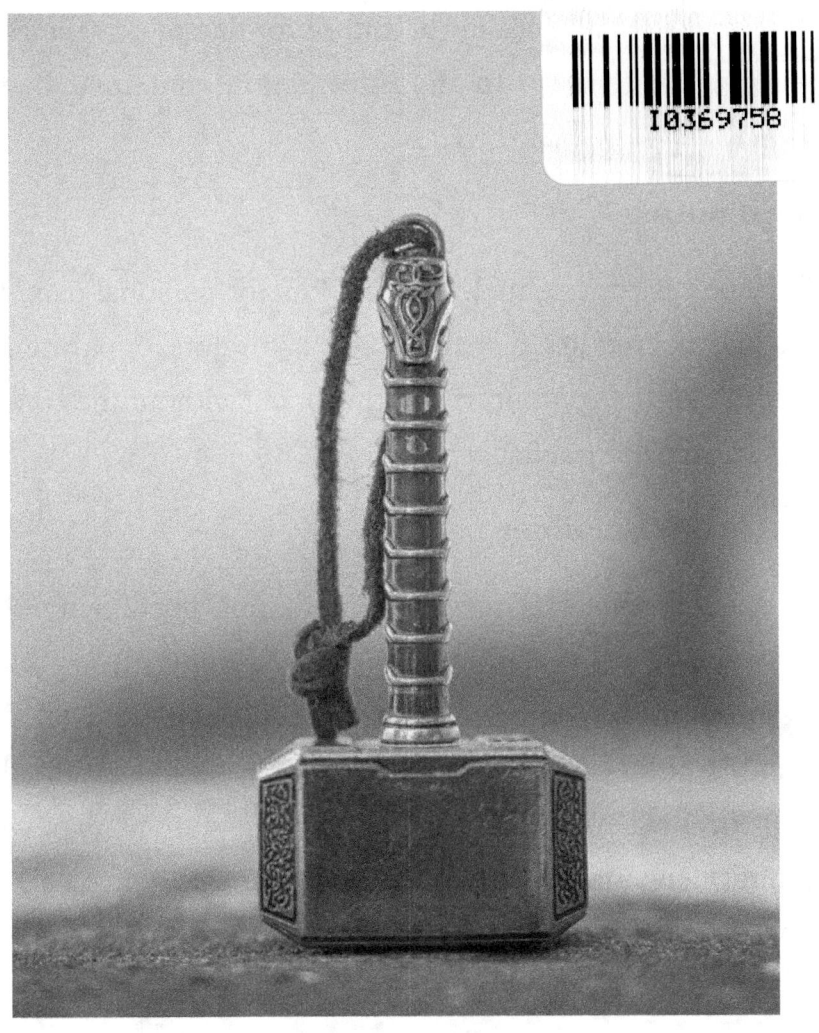

Aula Magna

© **Copyright 2023 Aula Magna - All Rights Reserved**

The contents of this book may not be reproduced, duplicated or transmitted without the written permission of the author or publisher.

Under no circumstances shall any legal fault or liability be attributed to the publisher or author for damages, repairs, or monetary losses due to the information contained in this book, directly or indirectly.

Legal notice

This book is copyrighted. This book is for personal use only. You may not modify, distribute, sell, use, quote, or paraphrase any part, or the content within this book, without the consent of the author or publisher.

Notice of disclaimer

Please note that the information in this document is for educational and entertainment purposes only. Every effort has been made to present accurate, up-to-date and reliable, complete information. No warranty of any kind is stated or implied. Readers acknowledge that the author makes no commitment to provide legal, financial, medical, or professional advice.

Table of Contents

Introduction

Chapter 1

Viking Origins 14

- The temple of Uppsala..................................22
- The eagle of blood..26
- The Viking calendar.......................................29

Chapter 2

Viking ships...34

- 2.1 The Karvi boat..36
- 2.2 Knarr..37
- 2.3 Snekkja..37
- 2.4 Skeid...38
- 2.5 Drakkar..38
- 2.6 Nydam's ship..39
- 2.7 Oseberg's Drakkar....................................40
- 2.8 Gokstad..40
- 2.9 Roskilde 6..40

Chapter 3

The Berserkers..41

Chapter 4

Stories about the creation of the world..................45

- 4.1 Ymir..................45
- 4.2 Day and night..................51
- 4.3 The sun and the moon..................52
- 4.4 The assistants of the moon..................52
- 4.5 The lineage of wolves..................53
- 4.5 The sea, the fire and the wind..................53
- 4.6 Hraesvelgr, the eagle of the winds..................54
- 4.7 Dvergar and the dwarf lineage..................55
- 4.8 The nine worlds..................55
- 4.9 The Yggdrasil, the tree of life..................60
- 4.10 The Bifrost, the rainbow bridge..................64
- 4.11 Hvergelmir and primordial rivers..................65

Chapter 5

Scandinavian deities..................67

Chapter 6

Asgard: The realm of the gods..................74

Chapter 7

The afterlife: Valhalla and Hel..................80

Chapter 8

The Principal Male Deities..87

- 8.1 Odin: the progenitor of all gods...............................87
- 8.2 The god Bragi...106
- 8.3 The god of deception: Loki....................................108
- 8.4 The mighty god of thunder: Thor..........................112
- 8.5 Týr... 114
- 8.6 Baldr...116
- 8.7 Heimdall...118
- 8.8 Vidarr.. 119
- 8.9 Forseti 120
- 8.10 Freyr..120
- 8.11 Hermod 120
- 8.12 Njǫrðr... 121
- 8.13 Mimir...121

Chapter 9

The Principal Female Deities...122

- 9.1 Iðunn 122
- 9.2 Freyja 124
- 9.3 Sif 125
- 9.4 Frigg 125

Chapter 10

The Ragnarök: the end of everything 128

Chapter 11

Scandinavian myths and legends..........136

- 11.1 The Deception of King Gylfi 136
- 11.2 The construction of Asgard..........140
- 11.3 The children of the god of deception Loki: Hel, Jormungandr, Fenrir 144
- 11.4 Thor vs. the giant Geirrøðr..........149
- 11.5 Thor, the stolen hammer and Freyja's unexpected marriage..........154
- 11.6 Thor vs. Hrungnir..........158
- 11.7 How Freyr lost his sword..........164
- 11.8 Baldr's death..........168

Introduction

Welcome dear reader, this is an in-depth introduction to Norse mythology, paganism (with its mystical settings) and all the interesting facts about the Viking people. This preamble will help us to better understand the succession of myths and legends from Scandinavia.

King Odin, the mighty thunder god Thor, the lowly Loki, and the Valkyries, before becoming the symbols of famous Marvel film transpositions, were the main characters of mystical and legendary realities from which artists-from Quorthon to Wagner from Robert E. Howard to Tolkien-of every age and period drew great inspiration. These "heroes" move within a universe of incredible beauty, magnificence and complexity ruled by the Yggdrasil. The Yggdrasil, which possesses a trunk capable of spanning all realms, is considered the mother tree of life; a symbol of the eternal, of what was and will be. Symbol of an ever-evolving life that joins earth and heaven in an inevitable and inescapable destiny. Simply put, the tree of life has a "mission" for every man, whose destiny is already written. It is important to point out major differences with revealed monotheistic religions: the Norse legends and myths were not revealed by one or more deities to man. The mythology of the North cannot be considered a religion in any way since it was not revealed (the main characteristic for a religion to be considered one). Rather, we could safely say, that mythology is a figment of human imagination.

It is curious that such myths, legends and various documentations came from Christian monks instead of pagan writers. The monks managed to save these tales from certain oblivion. These stories, which represent the traditional religion of Norse civilization, were, in fact, handed down orally before their Christianization. Although they were good carvers of metal, gold and wood for weapons and shields, they were unable to transcribe such stories because of their complexity. Too long and articulate were the exploits of the heroes to be able to report them with extreme fidelity.

It was to be, later, the Christians and Christianity that in addition to bringing the word of a monotheistic God taught the basics of using pen and paper. However, this is not to say that the Vikings were not able to pass on their deeds. In fact, the bards orally passed down the stories, myths and legends of their heroes through long poems.

The Edda, written by Snorri Sturluson around 1220, is the reference text for Norse mythology. An eclectic and very talented man, Snorri takes his inspiration very meticulously from pagan sources, in such a way as to preserve the enormous cultural heritage of his people by not altering it with the ethics and morals typical of the Christian religion. Snorri decides, therefore, to depart completely from the transcriptions of the Christian monks, who saw in the deeds of the Vikings demonic acts, exalting them instead, as heroic, virtuous and courageous.

But before we finally delve into the world of Norse mythology, it is necessary to take a very short but intense trip to Europe in search of the origins of paganism.

It all started with the Roman Empire and the various colonies to the north. The multitude of barbarian (especially Germanic) peoples lived on the fringes of the Empire, which although exerting great influence over them was unable to "convert" them and influence their customs and traditions. As soon as the kingdom began to crumble, between the 4th and 6th centuries CE, a large number of tribal alliances began to take control of the lands further north, no longer under the hegemony of Rome.

Two European superpowers were born as a result of these dismemberments: Merovingian France, and Anglo-Saxon England.

The Christian religion was able to expand exponentially, from the center outward. Almost all the peoples of northern Europe abandoned the old deities and embraced one God: the Christian God.

The Norwegian kings Olaf Tryggvason and Olaf the Holy, between the 10th and 11th centuries CE, implemented a strong

Christianization policy. Their rule was remembered because of bloody repression and persecution of pagans. History repeated itself, but in reverse parts, it was the pagans who were persecuted now and no longer the Christians. The pagans were burned alive, inside their temples with the statues of their idols. A new era began. Many of these pagans managed to flee to nearby Iceland, a kingdom without kings and religions, a fertile land to begin again to nurture the faint flame of paganism. A flame that was destined to be extinguished, however, because persecution of pagans began in Iceland in a very short time as well.

Denmark, from a bastion of paganism became, thanks to missionaries, a stronghold of Nordic Christianity.

Even the Swedes, who managed to maintain their traditions until 1164, were forced to go along with ecclesiastical power. Such was the power of the church that it managed to penetrate and conquer even Uppsala, Sweden's largest pagan agglomeration, a legendary stronghold, in the collective imagination, of the king of the Scandinavian gods: Odin.

Before this Christian capillarization, Vikings and paganism were considered one and the same. Sacrifice, devastation, and destruction were the cornerstone principles of the Viking peoples; the fear they instilled in the peoples they conquered was enormous. Since there were no official written histories that dictated in any way general guidelines for all pagan peoples, each tribe shaped its beliefs as it saw fit. In fact, the Scandinavian Pantheon, draws its origins from the Greek and Roman Pantheons but also from the monotheistic Christian religion.

"Scandinavian pantheon" refers to a very uniform set of cultures, ranging from the third millennium B.C. to the beginning of Christianity, united by the worship of the same gods.

With the advent of Christianity many customs and characteristics of the Scandinavian peoples disappeared but, amazingly, some of them managed to survive to the present day. Just think of the Norwegian calendar. Thursday, in fact, is called "Torsdag" in Norwegian and is derived from the mighty thunder god Thor. Not to mention Friday, which, again in Norwegian, is called "Fredag," referring to the fertility goddess, Frigg.

To best understand Scandinavian mythology, we must delve deep into their tales, myths and legends. We will learn about the sacks perpetrated in Germany, England, France, and Spain and how they were able to throw Christians into terror. Such was the Christian monks' fear of the Vikings that they depicted them almost as the weapon by which God used to punish them for their sins.

The terror perpetrated against European populations was not only due to violence and bloodshed. The Vikings, in fact, raided far more often than other populations did. Living mainly on islets and littorals, and lacking, therefore, the ability to expand their borders the only way to survive, was to raid. Sacking, therefore, was useful for two main reasons: to settle in more congruous areas and to procure provisions that were impossible to find in Scandinavia.

The Norse soon realized that it was better to establish real outposts in the raided lands rather than just sacking for its own sake. The main outposts of the Norse were the most raided lands ever: England and Ireland. The Norse from Norway settled in Ireland, giving birth to Dublin and making it a huge and wealthy city from the start. Their expansion into the Irish lands was short-lived, however; an alliance between the English and Danes was able to resist them and subsequently drive them out of Ireland.

To claim, however, that the Vikings were only bloodthirsty raiders would be dishonest and misleading. It is as clear as day that they were deadly, brutal, bloodthirsty warriors (at least that is how they appeared to the European peoples who suffered sackings, raids, and anguish of all kinds) but they were not just that. Norse culture is far less crude and uncouth than one might think. Their commanders were learned men of culture and great foresight: they worshiped the arts, myths and legends of warriors past. They adorned their battle fleets (famed for their speed, maneuverability, and pliability) with swords and shields not only to defend themselves but also to instill fear. They loved organization in everything they did and were witty traders. They were able to create large and dense trade networks and were respected for their wisdom and decision-making skills. Loyal and courageous leaders in battle, they hated restrictions on freedom but were able to have an iron discipline necessary to win battles.

Faith in their leaders came not from their subservience to them as commanders but from their respect for them. Respect gained in the field, showing themselves in every battle as valiant generals. To die in war, with hands soaked in the opponent's blood, was considered something absolutely valiant and respectable, a sure gateway to Walhalla(we will explain later what Walhalla was and consisted of).

We might therefore define the figure of the Norse warrior as that of a formidable and irreproachable hero, capable of great and unforgettable deeds but unable in turn to escape death. If we dig even deeper we will discover, even, that the warriors of the great north embraced death, espoused it, almost sought it out since to die in battle, with honor, meant having a place reserved at the banquet of the gods. The Vikings thought that nothing was forever and as soon as the fate of the gods materialized the end would come for everything and everyone.

It is precisely for this reason that in the narratives, the Scandinavian gods, unlike the Roman and Greek gods, were not thought to be immortal.

The fate of the gods was also yet to be fulfilled and the end of everything concerned them as well. The Ragnaröck(the end of everything and the beginning of everything according to Norse mythology) would be a great battle where most of the Gods would be killed and the whole of Asgard razed to the ground but would, finally, rise from its ashes. But now enough tergiversation, it is time to really begin our adventure. Let's dive into the mythical world of Scandinavian mythology together.

Chapter 1

Viking Origins

At the turn of 805 A.D. to 1112 A.D. the Scandinavian population (mostly from Norway and Denmark) decided to migrate, abandoning their lands, in search of fortune.

The Vikings were skilled navigators. For them, migrating, looting, raiding and fighting were common practices.

In the following centuries they established themselves as skilled traders. They were, even, able to make alliances in the palaces of power throughout Europe, in Russia but also in Iceland and Greenland pushing as far as the American continent. There is no certain data but it is assumed that they arrived in the Americas well before the Italian navigator and trader Christopher Columbus.

The term "Viking" comes from the Scandinavian languages, and etymologically speaking it is not used to represent a people with the same genetic origin. In fact, the term is descended from the word "vik," meaning bay, evidence of the maritime vocation of this people. So what bound these northern peoples together was an aptitude for work, for raiding and for always circumnavigating new seas. In this they identified themselves as Vikings. But there is more than just this hypothesis regarding the etymological origin of the name "Vikings." According to other scholars, the word from which

"Vikings" is derived is not "vik" but "vikja" which means to migrate, to go far, more precisely to move. We do not know the exact reason why the northern peoples decided to migrate from their lands.

In all likelihood, the increase in population and the inability to be able to exploit the resources of their cold moors prompted them to look for richer and more fertile places to continue to prosper. What we know with extreme certainty, however, is that in order to move as and where they wanted they needed boats that were fast, strong, and above all, resistant to the weather and vicissitudes they would undertake on their long journeys. These legendary boats were the "Drakkar."

If we dig even deeper, we will find that the Norse language is Germanic; this means that Franks, Lombards and Saxons (European barbarian peoples) spoke a language derived from the Norse language. In addition, the Germanic peoples who were already living in Europe for a very long time, namely the Franks, Saxons and Lombards, who surely came from Scandinavia, just like the Vikings, worshipped gods such as Odin and Thor.

As we mentioned earlier, the word "Viking" simply denoted men dedicated to raiding by sea and land; it had no particular ethnic connotation. The Vikings, therefore, could have been either Danish or Norwegian rather than Lappish. They had no state. They recognized and identified themselves in their customs rather than by their genetic or purely territorial descent. What made the Germanic barbarian populations, originally Norse who migrated to Europe, different from the Scandinavian ones was precisely the civilization they received from the Roman empire, both pagan first and Christian later.

The Vikings, in fact, disavowed the concept of "civilization" that the barbarian peoples, thanks to the Roman Empire, had acquired. One of the major reasons for interaction between the two peoples was trade and especially trade in furs. The Vikings were aware of the enormous amount of gold, hides and raw materials that Europe and the European peoples had at their disposal.

And that is exactly why in 792 A.D., the Norse attacked Lindisfarne, a small sacred island located on the coast of Northumberland,(if you are a fan of Netflix series and especially Vikings you know what we are talking about) in northeast England, where there was a very important monastery. This was exactly the moment when Europe realized the terrible threat that the Vikings would pose from there on. Lindisfarne's was the first Viking attack described and documented in a chronicle.

The Vikings who attacked the small island were most likely Norwegians. Although the small monastery was not razed, what caused a stir was the Vikings' behavior and total disregard for a sacred place. Until then, monasteries were not particularly guarded precisely because no one in battle would dare to attack priests and places of worship. It was this unscrupulousness on their part that threw the peoples of Europe into terror.

In the following years other monasteries were attacked in both Ireland and the Hebrides. But it was in 799 A.D. that the Vikings decided to get serious by pushing as far as the monastery of St. Philibert at Noirmoutier in mainland Europe. The raiding and sacking by the Vikings lasted for many, many years, especially in the English archipelago with a particular fondness for Ireland.

Given their aptitude for battle and penchant for victory, the Vikings also began to intervene in European civil wars by acting as a needle in family feuds over succession to the throne. Significantly, in fact, when Emperor Lothair I sought their help in defeating his brothers and establishing himself as sole heir to the throne.

But to see the first permanent settlements of Vikings in Europe will have to wait until the 9th century.

At the turn of the 9th and 10th centuries AD, the first Vikings to settle in Europe were the Norwegians. They settled permanently in Ireland, Scotland and England. Among the most famous founded cities were Dublin, Waterford and

Limerick. These cities were used as bases for raids into England and Ireland but also as important trading centers. In addition, the Norse had control of large parts of Scotland and some of its islands-Shetland, Orkney, and the Hebrides.

In 865 A.D. the Danish Vikings, thanks to a veritable army comparable to the major European powers, laid the groundwork for the conquest of all of England. They did not succeed in their intent until the end of the 9th. The chronicles of the time, in fact, told of a deadly army called "The Great Danish Army" that conquered almost all of England.

At that time, England as we know it today did not exist. It was an agglomeration of seven Anglo-Saxon kingdoms. The already feeble balance among the seven kingdoms was disrupted by the Danes, who in a very short time were able to conquer East Anglia (870) and Northumbria (867), dividing Mercia into several parts. Only and exclusively the kingdom of Wessex, thanks to an effective system of fortifications, was able to face them and subsequently repel them. Because of the defeats suffered by the kingdom of Wessex, the Danish army decided to settle further north in the kingdom of Northumbria, making York an important center for trade.

But it was not until the middle of the 10th century CE that the English were able to finally drive out the Danish Vikings. This was only possible thanks to the kingdom of Wessex, a bulwark against the Norse, which managed first to recapture all the

Anglo-Saxon kingdoms, previously conquered by the Vikings, and later to drive them out of England together with their King Eric, dubbed "the Bloody Axe." However, this was only the beginning because, as we would find out later, the Vikings would return very soon.

Under attack, however, was not only England but the whole of Europe, and throwing European populations into panic were not only Danish and Norwegian Vikings but also the Normans. The latter sacked cities such as Nantes, Paris, Orleans, and Tours reaching as far as Spain in Seville (controlled by the Arabs in 844), and in Italy in Pisa.

In 911 the Normans were the only Vikings to obtain a land grant from the then King of the Franks "Charles the Simple." They obtained portions of Neustria, more specifically the city of Rouen, and the surrounding territories. But to get all this, their leader Hrolfr (known as Rollo in Italian) had to impregnate himself to protect the whole area of the Seine by preventing and blocking access to other Norse. Thunderstruck by a somewhat dubious Christianity Rollone converted to Christianity, baptizing the following year and thus obtaining the office of Count of Rouen. The lands under his hegemony were all united under the same name: Normandy. To this day the collection of these lands is still called Normandy.

Later, around the year 1000, some Normans from the Altavilla family arrived in southern Italy, conquering land holdings near the areas of Capua and Melfi. Robert Guiscard, in 1059, became duke of Apulia and Calabria, and his brother, Roger I, succeeded in the feat of conquering Sicily, which until then had always been in Arab hands. A few years later, in 1130, Roger II - Robert's nephew and son of Roger I - was crowned king of Sicily, reuniting the Normans of southern Italy under a single kingdom.

As mentioned earlier, the 9th century was a period of great expansion for the Norwegian Vikings. First they came to Iceland (uninhabited at the time) then, to Greenland. There was no place that was so impassable that they were not conquered and raided. This was the great strength of the Vikings. Protagonist of these exploits was the great "Erik the Red." His son, Leif Erikson, being no less, even reached Newfoundland. These new lands were called "Vinland" or wine land by the Vikings. However, the first real confirmations of such tales, will only come in 1960, when near Anse Aux Medows were found the remains of an ancient Norse settlement that was apparently inhabited for only three years by Norwegian Vikings.

Instead, reaching the more remote parts of Eastern Europe were neither Norwegian nor Danish Vikings, but Norse from what is now Sweden.

They came to conquer most of the Slavic countries reaching, even, as far as Byzantium where they were known as "

Varianghi." The " Varianghi," Vikings from present-day Sweden, took a different attitude toward the subjugated peoples. More than as raiders and conquerors they behaved as traders, merchants and mercenaries. The Swedish Vikings attacked Constantinople (in 860) and later, in 940, Persia. It is even assumed, even, that the city of Kiev was founded by the Vikings, however, the sources are rather uncertain and scholars debated on this subject; therefore, it is fair not to take this information for absolutely true.

In the 10th century, "Blue Teeth," that is, King Harold II, converted to Christianity, succeeding in the feat of unifying Norway and Denmark under the sign of the Christian cross. Organized and united in religion, the Vikings returned to their interests in England. Succeeding in the feat, in 1013, was Harold II's deserter son, Sweyn Beardforcuta, who drove out and exiled the English king Aethelred II; but enjoying such a vast and strong empire was the son of "Beardforcuta," Harold II's grandson, namely, "Canute the Great" (Knut) who came to rule over a real empire encompassing present-day Norway, Denmark and England.

It was Edward "the Confessor," later in 1042, who regained England through the Anglo-Saxons. Harold II, for the short time he reigned, always managed to defend England from Viking raids. One of the most famous raids was that of the then former king of Norway, Harald III, who could do nothing against King Harold II's strenuous resistance. An England divided and in constant conflict was too great an opportunity not to be taken advantage of. Exploiting the situation, in fact, was the Duke of Normandy William, a powerful feudal lord of the King of France, who invaded England.

On October 14, 1066, at Hastings, a strenuous battle took place. The Normans defeated, once and for all, the Anglo-Saxons, killing King Harold II. The king of England became, at that point, William I "The Conqueror." Interestingly, it was a European of Viking descent who became ruler of England: the Norman William I.

It must, however, be stated that by now between the 10th and 11th centuries, the Vikings, whether Norwegian, Danish or Swedish, had established a different relationship with the subjugated peoples thanks mainly to Christianity; the days of raids and pillaging for their own sake were coming to an end.

1.1 The Uppsala Temple

Countless stories, myths and legends of the Vikings in pagan times. The last great pagan temple, the Uppsala Temple, was razed in the 11th with the advent of Christianity. The temple represented in toto what was the concept of paganism throughout Scandinavia.

Within the religious structure there was more than just religion. There was a strong connection between law and religion. In addition to including several mounds there were also schools and economic centers.

Indeed, war rituals in ancient civilizations were not only intended to win the battle but also to increase the prestige and rank of the combatant. The temple at Uppsala was completely gold-plated, and statues of the three most important deities in Norse mythology were praised: Odin, Thor and Freyr. Thor, the thunder god, occupied the throne in the center because of his strength. In fact, he was considered the strongest among the gods. On the sides, however, were Thor's father Odin and Freyr.

Thor, the god of thunder and lightning, of wind and rain but also of good weather and crops, lived in the heavens. His father, Odin, was in charge of war and infused men with strength to defeat their enemies. Freyr, on the other hand, granted peace and pleasure to men.

Not far from the temple was a very large tree with many branches whose leaves were always green even in winter. It was hard to tell which species it belonged to. Also in the vicinity of the tree was a well where bodies were thrown during rituals. If the bodies did not return to the surface, the people's wish could be granted.

The sacrifices the priests performed were on behalf of the people and were done to increase their prosperity. If plague, famine and famine were about to loom, the priests would implement actual sacrifices. In the case of famine and pestilence, sacrifices were made in the name of Thor, god of the earth. If one wanted to win in battle in the name of Odin, if one wanted to have luck in love in the name of Freyr.

Uppsala was, as mentioned earlier, not only a place of prayer and rituals but also a place of celebration. Every year, in fact, festivals and banquets were organized in which every small town in Scandinavia participated. No one excluded. The Uppsala temple had to be honored with gifts, even from the various kings of Scandinavia.

The modalities and rituals associated with the sacrifice were quite peculiar; nine heads dripping with blood (a symbol of fertility) were offered for each male living being. The bodies, however, were hung from the sacred tree, the Yaggdrasil, which was in the vicinity of the Uppsala temple.

The dances, feasts and sacrifices lasted for nine long days. Each day a different sacrifice. The sacrifices were all voluntary. To die in sacrifice or battle represented what was most noble for a Viking.

Archaeologists, however, are divided on whether Uppsala was an actual temple.

In Uppsala, it was not only the main deities who were paid homage. Rites and sacrifices were also made to the goddesses.

Such ceremony, which played a central role in Norse culture, was called "Disablot." Literally "Disablot" meant "sacrifice for the Goddesses"; scholars think of them as the three Nornir: Verðandi, Skuld and Urðr.

These rituals, according to scholars, were performed by the "blótgydja," a sacrificial priestess. The purpose of these sacrifices was to improve the neighbor, and increase the productivity of the land.

It should be remembered that the writers of the time were largely Christian and thus being totally unfamiliar with such cultures full of rituals and sacrifices may have misreported the sagas, myths and traditions of the Scandinavian people.

For this reason, historians are not, to this day, entirely convinced that the nature of Uppsala was that of a classical temple where worshippers were sacrificed but rather a kind of divine parliament where large statues of the gods held up the cosmos.

1.2 The blood eagle

Of all the myths and legends, stories of sacrifice and torture that of the Blood Eagle represents the most unique and shocking that has ever been handed down by Scandinavian culture. As mentioned earlier, the major translators and writers who translated and handed down the myths and stories of the Norse were Christian monks, who completely disowned a culture so distant from the Christian one, the pagan one indeed. It is therefore quite likely, we have reported inaccuracies precisely because of the non-affinity to the pagan world.

However, the dress often makes the monk, and certainly the Vikings were not puny fourth-rate warriors. They were tall, strong, almost indestructible, but above all, bloodthirsty warriors.

Blood was a central element in pagan culture, especially in Norse culture. Blood represented life. The branches and leaves of the sacred tree were flooded with the blood of those who willingly sacrificed in the name of the gods. In Scandinavian mythology everything was closely related to blood.

Blood, then, as the main element in both religious rites and death sentences. One of the cruelest and bloodiest Scandinavian death sentences ever was the "Blood Eagle."

It is said that one of its most illustrious vitte was indeed King Aelle of Northumbria.

But what did the blood eagle, also called "fire eagle," consist of? The prisoner was placed on his stomach with his face to the ground. An eagle was carved into the flesh after which with axe blows all the ribs were removed one by one and placed upward so as to look like an eagle. As the condemned person was skinned, the lungs were removed and placed on the ribs so as to increase the "eagle" effect. Finally salt was thrown into the wounds to increase the pain.

Scholars think the Vikings were so good at inflicting pain that the condemned remained conscious almost until the end of the torture.

One of the most disturbing aspects of this torture is that this practice was very common in Scandinavian daily life; a daily life punctuated by human sacrifices (whether for religious rites or death sentences).

King Aelle of Northumbria was not the only one to receive such an "honor." Many scholars claim that Halvdan Hålegg of Norway and the Irish ruler Máel Gualae also suffered the same fate. Although King Aelle's was certainly the most resounding.

If you have seen the TV series " Vinkings" you surely know who King Aelle was and how he died. Here historians report Aelle's death exactly as it is described by the director of

"Vikings." Deciding the fate of the King of Northumbria was the son of Ragnar Lothbrok i.e. Ivar Ragnarsson, the "Boneless." Ivar was intent on avenging his father's death that occurred at the hands of King Aelle who was guilty of locking Ragnar in a cell full of snakes, thus leaving him to certain death.

We have no definite accounts of the Blood Eagle. We do not know with absolute certainty whether it really existed as a method of torture. The only sources that mention the Blood Eagle reside in the "skaldic" poems. These poems are full of metaphors, similes and therefore difficult to interpret. One struggles to understand and comprehend the skaldic poems except in metaphorical form. Looking for historical truths in the skaldic poems could be a big mistake that Christian monks seemed not to care about. The latter translated such poems on the wave of emotions, sweetening the content as much as possible. The Christian world loved to describe and portray the Vikings as the armed arm of the devil.

1.3 The Viking Calendar

Unlike us, the Vikings did not use the four seasons. They divided the year into two seasons, summer and winter each with six months. They did not count the years cyclically as we do today, rather they began to count them only after major events. Northerners counted the months from full moon to full moon or new moon to new moon. Time was tracked by the Vikings through the moon. It was the moon that was the focus of their time management. Time was managed according to the moon and its movements.

The sun also played a central role in weather management since in addition to being a symbol of light and life it regulated crops.

Gormánuður, Ýlir, Mörsugur, Þorri, Goa and Einmánuður were the winter months and Harpa, Skerpla, Sólmánuður, Heyannir, Tvímánuður and Haustmánuður were the summer months.

The winter months

Gormánuður

It was the first of the winter months and was called the month of massacres. (October 14-November 13). On the first day a feast was held in Freyr's name to thank her for the harvest. This feast was called Veturnettr or Haustblót.

The Month of Jol was the second winter month; it is also known as Yule (November 14-December 13). It was in honor of Ýlir (one of Odin's many names). In this particular month of the year Odin traveled more than in other winter months and used to go from village to village getting to know the locals. Children used to put hay in their stockings for Odin's horse, Sleipnir. These tributes were made in the hope that Odin would give them small gifts in return. This month, the month of Yule, was dedicated to prosperity.

The third of the winter months was, literally translated, the "Bone Marrow Sucking Month" (Dec. 14-Jan. 12). This represented the month of the solstice.

Thorri was the fourth winter month. During this very month Torrablot was celebrated. On the night before the beginning of this month, a woman walked outside her house in search of Thorri to take him in and give him shelter. Thorri, by scholars, is framed as a Norse mythological figure, precisely the "son of snow" . Also in this month, men and women could choose any day to celebrate but if the chosen day coincided with a day of rain and bad weather it could be seen as a dark omen.

Goa

Goa was the fifth of the winter months (February 12-March 13) In all likelihood it was dedicated to Thorri's daughter. The month of Goa was famous for being the month dedicated to women where men engaged in caring for them.

The sixth and last of the winter months was Einmánuður.

This winter month was called "One Month" (March 14-April 13) and was dedicated to boys. March 21 is the spring equinox. During the month of Einmánuður fertility was celebrated.

The summer months

Harpa

This was the first of the summer months. (April 14-May 13). During the first day of the month the summer blót was held. The summer blót was nothing more than yet another sacrifice in the name of Odin. It was customary to do so to secure victories in battle and good luck in travel. Harpa was also the month dedicated to girls.

Skerpla

The second summer month was called Skerpla (May 14-June 12). The origin of the name "Skerpla" is unclear; scholars think it may refer to the concept of growth.

Sólmánuður

The third summer month was called the Month of the Sun (June 13-July 12). Summer Solstice Month, which mainly fell on June 21.

Heyannir

This was the fourth summer month and meant "Hay Harvesting" (July 13-August 14). It was the month of drying and harvesting hay.

Tvímánuður

This, however, was the fifth and penultimate summer month. (August 15-September 14). It symbolized the month of the grain harvest.

Haustmánuður

Last of the six summer months this also symbolized the harvest month (September 15-October 13). As we have seen, the Vikings were skilled farmers and, as such, totally dependent on seasonality.

Days of the Week

Most of the days, in the Viking calendar refer to names of Norse deities:

Sunday

Sunday was dedicated to the sun. It was also called Sunnudagr.

Monday

Monday, on the other hand, was the day dedicated to the moon and was called Mánadagr.

Tuesday

Tuesday was in homage to the god Týr called Týsdagr.

Wednesday

This day was also called Óðinsdagr. As can be easily inferred this day was dedicated to Odin.

Thursday

This was the day dedicated to the mighty thunder god Thor. Also called Þórsdagr.

Friday

This day was dedicated to Frigg or Freyja and was also called Frjádagr.

Saturday

Instead, this day was dedicated to bathing and was also called Laugardagr.

Chapter 2

Viking ships

Between the 9th and 13th centuries CE, the highest expression regarding naval technology of the time were the Viking boats. They were designed with the sole purpose of being fast, agile, light, and sturdy. They were perfect both for plowing long distances at sea and for sailing up rivers and large streams where the water was much shallower. It was thanks to these boats that the Vikings were extremely successful in naval battles. Moreover, such boats enabled them to make stealthy and sudden raids to catch by surprise and put enemies in great difficulty who were not used to facing warriors as hostile as the Vikings.

The ships used by the Vikings were mainly of two types: warships and trading ships. Those for war had to be fast agile and sturdy for the reasons explained above. Those for trade, on the other hand, had to be, first and foremost, capacious to increase cargo capacity at every single leg, and tough for voyages potentially full of pitfalls.

The ships used by the Vikings to descend into battle were not true warships similar to modern battle boats. They were mostly considered troop transport ships. This type of ship represented a major advantage. In fact, the Vikings used them as floating platforms by means of which they then attacked the enemy, as if they were on dry land, through the use of axes and swords. No heavy weapons or rostrums to destroy the enemy's boats; the Vikings did not need them. The technique used by the Vikings in naval clashes was as unique as it was effective.

The hull of Viking ships, which were used in warfare, was long, thin and light with a draft often less than a meter which enabled them to overcome shallow water but more importantly to land on any kind of beach by simply dragging the boat ashore. Generally the ratio there was between length and width was 7 to 1.

The symmetrical structure was a major feature of many Scandinavian ships (except those used for trade or long sea voyages). The stern and bow were virtually equal and allowed for easy, agile, and dynamic handling of the boat, thus enabling circular maneuvers necessary for sudden course changes.

Lightning fast course changes, for example, were necessary when icebergs and ice were encountered at sea. Such maneuvers were only possible with vessels designed and structured in this way.

Sail and oars were the main methods of propulsion for warships. On the open sea, sails were used because they allowed much faster travel than the use of oars and were ideal for covering long distances. Again thanks to sails, the crew could avoid making unnecessary efforts, thus conserving energy for battles.

As we mentioned earlier they were exceptional vessels. Scholars claim that sails could be hoisted or lowered very quickly. The estimated time to hoist or lower a sail was about 90 seconds

The ships were not equipped with rowing benches. For this reason, the crew, in order to save space sat on crates that held their personal belongings. The size of the crates allowed an oarsman to sit at the right height so that he could maneuver the oar as congruously as possible.

The hull structure was incredibly innovative (for that time) and allowed for staggering speeds. Average sailing was about 9-18 km/h but, in optimal environments, a Scandinavian ship could reach a top speed of almost 30 km/h.

Viking ships are usually classified according to hull characteristics or construction details. However, it is the rowing stations that are the most commonly used method of judging vessels.

2.1 The Karvi boat

Of all Viking boats the Karvi was certainly the smallest. To be considered a "Karvi" type boat, boats had to have at least 13 oar spaces (although Vikings used to classify boats with fewer oars as "Karvi" as well)

The length-to-width ratio was 4: 5: 1. Their purpose was to be multifunctional ships, capable of both warfare and trade. The evolution of this type of vessel into the "Knarr," allowed for long ocean voyages during the Viking expansionist era.

2.2 Knarr

Knarr-type vessels were used for long sea voyages and trade. The hull was wider, deeper and shorter than that of the mounted on armored ships (with a width-to-length ratio very similar to that of karts), all of which made such vessels spacious, dynamic and maneuverable even with a small crew. At 16 meters long and five meters wide, the Knarr were capable of carrying more than 23 tons of cargo. It was thanks to these types of ships that Scandinavian peoples explored the Mediterranean, far and wide, reaching as far as the Baltic Sea and bringing supplies to even the most extreme colonies far from the Atlantic Ocean such as Iceland and Greenland.

2.3 Snekkja

The Snekkja was a small, light, military-style boat, which had no less than 20 seats for rowers on board. This formidable vessel was capable of carrying up to 41 men. It was approximately 17 meters long and 3 meters wide and equipped with a draft of only half a meter. Of all military ships the

Snekkia was the most common. However, not all Snekkia-type military vessels were equal to each other. Those of the Norwegian type, for example, had a deeper draft than those of the Danish type. The reason for this was dictated by the fact that the Norwegian ones had to be able to easily cross the fjords and overcome the harsh Atlantic climate without too much worry.

Another of the special features of these formidable ships was that they did not need to dock in ports. In fact, they were simply washed ashore or beached. They were so light that often to cross small stretches of land the Vikings carried them on their shoulders, thus allowing "arm" transport.

2.4 Skeid

They were larger battle boats than the Snekkja and were equipped with no less than 30 seats for rowers. Aboard a Skeid one could easily get about 70 to 80 men, while the length, however, was at least 30 meters. One of the longest Skeids was the "Roskilde 6" which was discovered in 1996, dating back to the year 1051. It was 37 meters long.

2.5 Drakkar

When we think of Viking vessels we think of ships adorned in the hull with carved arches in the shape of beasts. Indeed, the special feature of these ships, as well as, the only real big difference with the Skeids was just that: the hull and its decoration, which often coincided with carved bows in the shape of dragons or snakes. The reasons for such decorations in the Drakkars are still not entirely clear but it seems they had a dual purpose: to frighten enemies but more importantly to keep the sea monsters that inhabited the cold northern waters at bay. Clearly, all we know about the Drakkars is due to transcriptions of myths, stories and legends that have always been part of the Norse universe.

Absolutely certain truths, speaking of the Vikings and their exploits, we have none, but the information we have about their ships is quite true and reliable.

Having examined the various types of Scandinavian boats let us go into a little more detail by seeing which of these were the most famous:

2.6 Nydam's ship

A wooden vessel that could weigh up to three tons. Its discovery dates back to the years 310-320 AD. The ship was 23 meters long and 4 meters wide and could hold up to 15 pairs of rowers.

2.7 Oseberg's Drakkar

Considered more of a Karvi than a Drakkar, she was 21 meters long and 5 meters wide, the mast, however, was about 10 meters. The sail had a surface area of about 90 square meters and allowed the ship to reach a speed of nearly 10 knots. The ship was used for the burial of two women whose identities remain a mystery.

2.8 Ship of Gokstad

The largest Norwegian Viking ship ever discovered was the Gokstad in the 9th century. The ship is about 23.80 meters long

and about 5 wide. It was capable of carrying up to 32 oarsmen. The maximum speed of this vessel was about 12 knots.

2.9 Roskilde 6

The Roskilde 6 was by far the largest Scandinavian vessel ever built. It was found in Denmark, more specifically in Roskilde, and its length was an impressive 37 meters.

Chapter 3

The Berserkers

Not all Viking warriors were the same, among them the Berserkers stood out in strength and violence. They were formidable and bloodthirsty pagan warriors devoted to Odin. They dressed in bear or wolf skins. Tenacity, temper, courage, and strength were just some of the virtues of these incredible warriors. The protagonists of the ancient Norse sagas were just that. Being a Norse warrior meant braving the stormy seas, plundering, killing and torturing without remorse, for, again according to their culture, only the strongest were worthy to live.

Viking society was based on violence. Even today when we hear of Norse myths and sagas we think of bloody and violent battles to the last breath. They were certainly not an anarchic society, yet it was certain and common knowledge that the cardinal principles of their society were war and violence. Violence was primarily used to enforce laws.

The Vikings had a dense and rigid system of laws and rules that often referred to honor as well. Wars, although bloody and brutal, were the ideal place to stand out and become famous and coveted. Such practices were regulated by unwritten codes.

As we mentioned earlier, there was a type of Norse warrior that went far beyond the concept of a simple warrior. Berserkers were considered almost gods closer to the world of gods and beasts than to the human world. Etymologically speaking, the term "Berserker" is derived from "berr," which meant bear, and "sakr," which meant mesh. Combining the two terminologies thus came to form the term Berserker or "man with bear's clothing, beast's clothing."

The Berserkers were holy men. Their entire existence was devoted to the worship of Odin. At first, in the early days of Scandinavian society, Berserkers lived far from population centers, usually in totally uninhabited areas where they could hunt and make sacrifices in the name of the gods, mainly to Odin. Viking armies consisted mainly of these formidable warriors and the Berserkers. As they began to sail with the raiders and thus reached all over Europe, their reputation as cruel and ruthless killers grew by leaps and bounds, especially in England. Bear warriors were feared by all in battle. Sometimes their armor was composed only of bear furs. Those of them who used wolf heads instead were called ulfheðnar, or "wolf heads." They had no rules in battle. The only rule, if we can call it that, was to kill and raid as much as possible without any remorse or regret.

The reason they fought so strenuously and were so violent was due to the massive doses of drugs, which could eliminate the sense of fatigue, exhaustion and pain from their minds. This state of complete self-alteration was called Berserkesgrang (becoming Berserker). This stage of hallucination was attainable only by the average use of hallucinogenic fugus mixed with massive intakes of alcohol.

The euphoria from the mix of mushrooms and alcohol made them almost invincible in battle. They did not feel the cold, wounds and had an irrepressible urge to fight; such was the frenzy of battle that they often attacked even their own comrades. The mere presence of a Berserker was enough to instill so much fear in their enemies. Their exploits were so famous that they were often hired as personal guards by Scandinavian kings. Given the prolonged use of alcohol and hallucinogenic mushrooms, the altered state could last for days. This was not at all healthy for the Berserkers, who ended up going mad, suffering from epilepsy attacks or even dying. Uncontrolled and unwarranted outbursts of fury against their comrades could also be a side effect.

To charge into battle, they used to howl and bite their shields. They were feared by everyone, even by their own comrades who did everything to avoid them. At the end of battles, the Berserkers, preferred to stay outside the so-called "civilized" areas since they did not recognize themselves in any order or law. They were true beasts; the only law they worshiped to follow was violence. With the advent of Christianity these diehard pagan warriors ceased to exist. Too difficult, uncouth and bloodthirsty to be converted; so they disappeared along with their pagan deities and a society that gave way to Christian values. They remained alive only in myths, poems and legends, imperishable manifestos of their adventures.

Chapter 4

Scandinavian stories about the creation of the world

4.1 Ymir

In the mists of time, before everything was created, nothing was as we know it today. There was no earth, no sky, no sea. There were no plants, animals or human beings. The primordial aspect of the entire universe, according to Scandinavian beliefs, was nothing but infinite oblivion. A dark mass, a cosmic nothingness represented by chaos and powerful energies. This dark, formless black hole-like mass was called Ginnungagap

To the north of Ginnungagap could be found the dark region of permanent ice, where frost and fog characterized the entire region, referred to as "Niflheim" the "house of fog"; farther south, however, arose the Muspellsheim, a fiery territory characterized by blazing flames and unbearable heat. Lava in this portion of Ginnungagap reigned supreme.

In the center of the Niflheim, there was a well, the Hvergelmir, from which flowed the ancestral streams, called Élivágar, which bubbled and thundered at very high temperatures. There were eleven in all and they were called Svol, Gunnthra, Fjorm, Fimbulthul, Slidr, Hrid, Sylgr, Ylgr, Vid, Leiptr and Gjoll. Legend has it that these rivers fell into Ginnungagap, creating immense icy waves which filled the entire Ginnungagap with thick icy foam.

The eleven rivers went so far from their original source that the toxic substance, due to combustion, hardened into an ice slag. A light rain, which turned into frost, fell over the entire Ginnungagap covering it with a peculiar layered ice.

These were the events that led to the birth of the universe and the Norse gods. Two opposite poles, ice on one side and fiery moors on the other, but absolutely complementary.

Rivers of ice, coming from Niflheim, and of lava, coming from the fiery land of Muspellsheim, continued to meet and flow into the void Guinnungagap. From the 'union of these two types of rivers, particles of molten frost with life inside were created.

The fusion of these two streams, one of lava and one of fire, gave birth to two beings: Ymir the father of giants, a huge humanoid with androgynous features capable of towering over the entire world, and a cow called Auðhumla, whose job it was to feed him.

Everything could be thought of except that Ymir was good; he was as wicked as all his descendants. The reason for his wickedness lay in his birth. The drops of life from which Ymir was born, sprayed by the Elivagar, contained poisonous particles. It was these particles that made Ymir and all his descendants evil.

Although gigantic, he was only an infant and as such his only concerns were eating and sleeping. Not being able to unite with one of his kind he decided of his own free will to beget children.

Ymir slept, was very tired and began to sweat very conspicuously. From the perspiration escaping from his right arm a pair of giants were born: a male and a female. From the sweating of the legs, however, was born Þrúðgelmi: a giant endowed with six heads famous for giving birth to Belgermir.

Adhumula, the cow, fed herself by licking salt from the frozen stones present in Niflheim. On the first day, as the sun went down, she first gave birth to man's hair, then on the second day the head and on the third day the whole body.

This being was the first of the gods, his name was Buri, and just like Ymir he had androgynous features. Beauty and strength were not his only qualities. She gave birth to a son, Bor, who conjoined with Bestla, a giantess daughter of Blalþorn, one of the many giants born of Ymir. Three sons were born of their union. Odin, was the name chosen for the firstborn, Vili for the second and Vé for the third.

Odin, Vili and Vé - began a bloody battle against Ymir. With a powerful axe blow to the head they succeeded in killing him and exposed his body in the middle of Guinnungagap.

Out of Ymir's carcass came worms to which Odin and his brothers transmitted knowledge and consciousness. Thus it was that the worms changed into dwarfs going to dwell in the bowels of the earth becoming great craftsmen in the service of the gods. Craftsmen so good that they forged the great treasures of the gods.

From the lifeless body of Ymir, they created the whole world. From flesh they made earth, from bones they made mountains. From the teeth, jaws and splinters of bones they made boulders and rocks. From hair they created forests, and from his brain, throwing it into the air, they created clouds.

They placed Ymir's huge skull above the sky, which was divided into four parts. They placed at the four corners of the sky four dwarves-Austri, Vestri, Nordri and Sudri-who had the task of supporting it. The names of the four dwarfs indicated the four cardinal points.

From the blood of Ymir, gushing from the giant's wounds, the sons of Bor created the ocean. In this ocean sprung from Ymir's blood they drowned all the giants.

After that, the entire world was raised from the depths and the three deities created the place destined for the giants, the Jotunheim, located at the far end of the earth.

Thereafter, the world of men was created, protected by mighty fortifications generated by Ymir's eyebrows. This realm was called Midgard, the middle realm.

The three brothers were able to drown all the giants descended from Ymir, but the only ones saved were Bergelmir and his wife.

It is not easy to understand how Bergelmir managed, along with his wife, to save himself. Some scholars say that he succeeded by climbing to the top of a mill, thus escaping the deluge of blood. Others, however, claim, that he used a hollowed-out log as a boat.

Regardless of what one thinks about Bergelmir's escape, the two giants managed to save themselves, took refuge in the Jotunheim, and gave birth to the descendants of the frost giants, the Jotnars.

Subsequent to the creation of the world, the three deities collected the particles of life floating in the sky, ejected from the Múspellsheimr, placing them in the center of Guinnungagap, to radiate light not only to the earth but also to the sky.

The moon and sun in those days wandered in total freedom in the heavens, unaware of what their functions and potentials were. The same fate befell the stars, which wandered without any point of reference. It was Odin, together with his sons, who gave an order to the firmament, reserving for all the stars a location and task. Some stars fixed, in the vault of the sky, while others were given a course to follow. They gave the course of the sun a designation for the morning and one for the evening but also one for noon and one for the afternoon. They were able to measure the phases of the moon by imposing a motion and a time. They created the "gears" of the firmament, giving balance in every part of the universe. By doing so they were able to calculate the time of days months and years; it was through this cosmic reorganization that the calculation of time thus began.

4.2 Day and night

Norfi was a giant who lived in Jotunheim. His daughter was named Nótt (night), was dark and had brown eyes just like every member of her race. She was forced to marry bride Naglfari. From their union was born a son named: Authr. Later, she married Annarr and from their union was born Jord (earth). Finally, she married Dellingr and from their union was born Dagr (day).

To celebrate, the gods, took Nótt and Dagr, gave them two steeds, fast enough to complete a full circle of the earth in only 12 hours, and two fantastic chariots. They placed Nott and Dagr in the sky so that they could complete a circle of the earth every day. Nott was the first to circle the earth with his horse Hrimfaxi, also called "frost mane." Every morning, the foam from Hrimfaxi's bite would drip onto the earth, generating dew showers in the moors. In contrast, Dagr's steed, Skinfaxi, was nicknamed "shining mane." Heaven and earth were flooded with the shimmering splendor of his mane. With every stride he took in the sky, the world lit up.

4.3 The Sun and the Moon

One day, a man named Mundilfari had two children. The beauty of the two little ones was so dazzling that he decided to give them two important names. The male child was named Mani, the female child Sol.

Jealous, impatient and full of pride at seeing a human take over the name of their creations, the gods captured both sons Mani and Sol and took them to heaven. Sol, was placed at the head of the chariot carrying the sun, a chariot previously built by the gods to illuminate the world. Árvakr and Alsvithr were the horses assigned to pull the chariot. Two iron bellows were placed under the horses' shoulder blades to cool them down once they began their gallop. Svalinn was the name of the shield that was placed in front of the sun. Máni was responsible for the movements of the moon, as well as the rise and fall of its phases.

4.4 The helpers of the moon

Bil and Hjuki were two young boys who were the sons of Vithfinnr. One night they decided to wander away from Byrgir's well, taking with them a staff named Simul and an old bucket named Saeg. At one point Mani, the deity in charge of transporting the Moon in her chariot, abducted them, taking them with her to the Moon. Mani was the deity opposite to Sol. Sol, his sister, instead transported the Sun in a chariot). Mani made up his mind to abduct them when he realized that the two young men were perfect for regulating the various phases of the Moon.

4.5 The lineage of wolves

An elderly orca lived in the Iron Tree Forest in Jarnividr, east of Midgard. Bored with the way she spent her days, she decided to create wolf-like giants and raise them.

Thus were born Fenrir, Skoll, Hati and Managarmr the moon dog. The latter was stronger and more mighty than all, even Fenrir. Legend has it that Managarmr, at the end of the world, the Ragnarock, would eat the flesh of men, swallow the moon and smear the earth and sky with blood.

4.5 Wind, sea and fire

The progenitor lineage of the world, were the giants. Considered to be very wise beings, they had full control over every element of creation.

It is said that Fornjótr, a very old giant, had control over the cold and frozen moors of Finnland. His descendants were strong and famous progeny: Aegir, Logi and Kari.

Aegir was the god of the seas. He was married to Ran. He possessed a large net with which he collected drowned people and transported them to his home. The waves of the sea were represented by his nine daughters. Aegir's daughters were famous for their beer, so good and fresh that all the gods gathered in one of their rooms to drink and toast.

Logi, on the other hand, represented fire. His full name was Halogi, meaning "burning flame." He was the ruler of "Halogaland," a province named after him.

Kári represented the wind. He had a son named Frost, or he who was able to master ice and cold; his son was called Snær, the snow. The latter had four sons, Þorri, Fǫnn, Mjǫll and a daughter, Drífa.

Þorri was the "month of the fourth wind," Fǫnn, on the other hand, represented "sleet," while Mjǫll was "fresh snow" and Drífa was "snowstorm."

Many scholars actually claim that Logi and Skjálf (his sister) were descended from Frost. The two avenged their father as Agni, ruler of the Ynglingar, killed him.

4.6 The Hraesvelgr eagle: queen of the skies

In the northernmost reaches of the heavens lived a giant called Hræsvelgr with features resembling those of an eagle. When he flapped his huge wings he was able to create whirlwinds of air so strong that they swept over the whole world. The winds that blew over the world were derived from the movement of his mighty wings.

4.7 Dvergar and the Dwarf lineage

Do you remember how the dwarves were born? They were worms present in Ymir's dead flesh. Ymir's blood was transformed, later into water and the bones into rock. From the blood was born Brimir and from the bones Blainn

In the bowels of the earth took up residence the dwarves of the Dvergar lineage. Among them, one stood out in wisdom and strength: Motsognir. Another great dwarf of the Dvergar dynasty was Durinn; created to bring back the deepest secrets of the dwarf kingdom.

Other famous Dvergar were Sudri, Nordri, Vestri, and Austri: four small dwarves able to hold up the sky at its four cardinal points. Later came Nýi and Níði to rule new moon and full moon.

4.8 The Nine Worlds

Following Ymir's sacrifice, which was necessary for the creation of the new universal order, it was the Æsir who took control. As soon as Ymir died, from his dismembered flesh, the universe was born and from the skull the vault of heaven. Sól and Máni (the Sun and Moon) infused light and warmth, managing the passage of time. The entire universe was surrounded by an immense outer ocean (úthaf) created by the universal deluge of blood caused by the slaughter of the first giants; the timeless giants.

In the middle of the universe was Midgard, also referred to as an "inner recitation," where mankind, the human sons of Askr and Embla, resided. To protect humans from the jotnars, the cold giants and descendants of Bergelmir, the gods designed a wall created from the eyelashes of the deceased giant Ymir. The Jotnairs lived outside in Utgard, which represented the end of the world; it was located near the cosmic ocean.

Various deities, including Alfars, and Dvergar along with other beings, dwelt in other lands, in the deepest bowels of the world or in the most impervious regions of the heavens. According to the learned, there were nine worlds. The Élivágar were cosmic rivers that flowed from the source of Hvergelmir and passed through each of these nine worlds, representing a veritable junction between them.

Yggdrasil, the great ash tree, was considered the tree of life.

Its stem was the main pivot that joined earth to heaven, its branches covered the vault of heaven, and its roots were able to reach the various worlds: that of deities, the dead, and men.

The nine kingdoms all resided within the Yggdrasil. Its branches and roots were the homelands of various kinds of beings: the human race, the giants and all the deities. But to everything there is a beginning and an end. Each of these nine kingdoms would be destroyed by the end of the whole, represented in Scandinavian mythology by the Ragnarök.

The middle enclosure, the first of the nine worlds, was the Midgard, which was located at the center of the universe. Within the Midgard resided men. Just below the realm of men was Asgard, the main city of Odin's kingdom, Ásaheimr. These two worlds were joined by the Bifrost, the rainbow bridge. The world of humans was surrounded by an insurmountable ocean. This narrow and impassable ocean was inhabited by the legendary Jormungandr, a giant sea monster in the shape of a serpent. According to Norse mythology, this serpent surrounded the entire Midgard from one end to the other by biting its own tail.

The Æsir, then, came from Ásaheimr, whose main city was Asgard, full of magnificent temples and majestic buildings. The ruler of the Æsir was Odin. Asgard was located in the heavens, and because of this privileged position Odin, sitting on his Hliðskjálf throne, was able to observe and notice whatever was happening in all nine realms. Valhalla represented the afterlife for the Vikings. Only the most deserving could enter it, only those who had died with honor and glory in battle. The latter was located at the gates of Asgard.

Vanaheimr, was the third world and was inhabited by the Vanir. The Vanir were master sorcerers who could predict the future. Scholars place this world to the west of Ásaheimr (there is no definite data on the location).

The fourth kingdom was that of the Jotnar (a race of giants sworn enemies of the Æsir). Its name was: Jotunheim. Jotunheim was located at the far end of the world, in Utgard. It was an extremely impervious place made up of rocks, frozen deserts and impassable forests.

The light elves, the Ljósálfar, lived in the fifth world called Álfheimr. The world of the Ljósálfar was very close to that of the Æsir. These fantastic beings, were regarded as guardian angels. They were minor deities of nature and fertility who were highly valued by humans since they helped them with their magical powers and knowledge. They were devoted not only to magical arts but also to art and music.

Underground, in the deepest bowels, was the sixth world, Svartálfaheimr. This underwater world was inhabited by the Dvergar and the Døkkálfar, their ruler was Hreidmar. These beings were masters of craftsmanship. They were able to create and later give as gifts many objects for the gods of Asgard. Such as the Gungnir, the mythical and legendary spear of Odin.

Niflheim, was the seventh world and was by far the coldest and darkest region. Considered the home of fog, darkness and primordial ice. Niflheim was a far more impervious and cramped place than Jotunheim. Originally part of Ginnungagap, it was one of the oldest worlds.

In opposition to the Niflheim was the eighth world, the fiery Múspellsheimr, also initially part of the Ginnungagap. The eighth world was as inhospitable as the seventh. The environment was rendered uninhabitable not by bitter cold but by scorching fire, lava covering the ground, flames leaking from cracks in the earth, and soot making the surrounding air unbreathable.

The ruler of Múspellsheimr was the giant Surtr. This eighth kingdom was inhabited by fire giants. Surtr hated Odin and was his sworn enemy. In fact, when Ragnarök, "the end of the world," came, Surtr would ride out on his horse and with his flaming sword dripping with lava would attack the Æsir kingdom and Asgard, destroying it and turning it into a living hell.

The last realm, the ninth world, was that of Hel. A very dark and cramped place it was ruled by Hel, daughter of Loki. To experience happiness within that place was virtually impossible; no Viking would ever succeed. The ninth world was the "home" of all swindlers, thieves and murderers who had died dishonorably. They were not eligible to go to Valhalla to feast with the gods.

It was located in the most remote and darkest part of the entire universe. Rain, frost and fog were a constant in the ninth world. Beneath Hel's realm was Niflhel, an arid fog-filled hell. Evil souls, passed through Hel , were thought to go right into the Niflhel.

Except for Midgard, the world of humans, all others were invisible worlds that could manifest themselves in some aspect of the visible world (Jotunheim with the physical desert, Hel with the tomb, and Asgard with the sky).

The Æsir, once they had created the universe, decided to build their fortress, Asgard, on top of very high mountains that were virtually inaccessible.

The gods made Asgard an idyllic place by constructing magnificent temples, houses and buildings. Once the construction of Asgard was finished, Odin chose twelve gods who would rule and protect the kingdom together with him.

4.9 The Yggdrasil, the tree of life

As we mentioned earlier, Yggdrasil represented the tree of life. Its trunk united heaven and earth, and its branches with its branches represent the lifeblood of the nine kingdoms. It was the mightiest and strongest of trees; an evergreen symbol of what is good and what is evil. It represented the eternal flow of life. A powerful metaphor capable of uniting heaven and earth in one irreversible and inescapable destiny. Its very long branches stretched over all the worlds until they entirely covered the heavens. Drops of honey, like dew, fell from these branches onto the earth, allowing bees to feed on them. There were three roots capable of supporting this mighty tree of life which, in turn, branched out in three different directions.

The first of the three roots reached into the remotest depths. Some scholars claim that it reached as far as Helheimr, the territory of the non-living, while many others, however, claim it extended as far as Niflheim, thus reaching the source of Hvergelmir. Under this root hid the dangerous and much-feared serpent Nidhogg.

The second root headed, however, toward Jotunheim, land of the ice giants, reaching as far as the spring of Mímisbrunnr. This was the place of wisdom and knowledge, and Mimir was the keeper and owner of such a well. It was Mimir who allowed Odin to drink from the spring thus assuming unparalleled knowledge and wisdom. But to do so Odin had to pay a very steep bill: to sacrifice his eye as a token. So the father of the gods compromised and to attain supreme wisdom and knowledge he bartered his eye with the well keeper Mimir.

The third, and final root, on the other hand, reached as far as Ásaheimr by reaching the eternal spring of Urdarbrunnr, a place where the Æsirs held daily meetings. In front of the spring, just below the ash tree, was a magnificent dwelling where the Nornir Urd, Verdandi and Skulld lived. The latter were the only ones who could take care of the mighty tree by watering it with a miraculous water that kept it healthy, alive and flourishing.

In that miraculous spring also lived two swans. It was from these two swans that this wonderful species began.

On the summit of the Ásaheimr Mountains stood a huge eagle, keeper of ancient secrets, whose beating wings gave rise to winds so strong that they could sweep the world of humans. This mighty bird incessantly surveyed the horizon to warn the gods of possible incoming enemies.

Beneath the roots of the mighty ash tree were horrible and fearsome serpents, Móinn and Góinn, twins and firstborns of Grafvitnir, but also Grafvǫlluðr, Grábakr, Sváfnir and Ófnir. However, the most dangerous was surely Nidhogg, in constant and incessant struggle with the eagle. Each of these beings gnawed, never stopping, at the roots of Yggdrasil. Acting as the messenger between the two beings, between the eagle and the snake was Ratatoskr, a friendly squirrel who reported any provocation the two animals exchanged. The duel between the giant eagle and the huge snake Nidhogg metaphorically shows in toto the incessant struggle between good and evil. A struggle between light and darkness, between ignorance and wisdom destined never to end.

But feeding on the leaves and branches of Yggdrasil were not only the beings we have listed so far; there were also four mighty and wise deer called: Dáinn, Dvalinn, Duneyrr and Duraþrór.

And it is precisely for this reason that the work of the Nornir became of paramount importance to prevent the leaves and roots of the sacred ash tree from drying out, decreeing its demise.

But Yggdrasil was not the only sacred tree. Historians speak of at least two others besides the sacred ash tree: one was called Léraðr and the other Mímameiðr.

The deer Eikþyrnir and the goat Heiðrún fed on the leaves of Læraðr. This sacred deer was located in Valhalla. From its horns gushed drops so large that they formed, in the deepest bowels of the world, the well of Hvergelmir. From here all the rivers in the universe had their origin.

On the other hand, the goat Heiðrún, on the roof of Valhalla, grazed effortlessly above the foliage of the huge ash tree. The mead on which the einherjar fed flowed from the very udders of this sacred goat.

Meanwhile, Víðófnir the rooster, bitter rival of the giants, waited to pronounce on Ragnarök: he would unveil, without hesitation, its coming.

According to many scholars of Norse mythology, however, it is believed that Læraðr and Mímameiðr were nothing more than Yggdrasil but with different names.

4.10 The Bifrost, the rainbow bridge

The Bifrost, the rainbow bridge, represented the passage, the point of conjunction, of union between earth and sky. It was the gods who built this magnificent bridge, thanks to their profound wisdom. But the passage was not easy; only those with certain qualities could use the Bifrost.

Guarding the bridge was a sentinel chosen by the gods: Heimdallr. His task, as delicate as it was important, was to guard, night and day, access to the Bifrost, preventing the arrival of giants who, once there, might attempt to climb the sky until they reached the gates of Asgard.

Although it might have looked fragile, the rainbow bridge was solid and of fine workmanship. It was meant to last until the end of the world and would collapse once the Ragnarök came. The Ragnarök would spare nothing in the universe, including Bifrost.

The various deities traveled over the rainbow bridge Bifrǫst every day to travel to the source of Urdarbrunnr. They used to hold their assemblies near Yggdrasil; considered an ideal place as it was mystical.

Interestingly, passage over the bridge was denied to Odin's son Thor, the god of thunder, as the whole Bifrǫst would have gone up in flames under the mighty wheels of his chariot.

Therefore, to pass over the Bifrost, Thor had to give up his chariot by going on foot.

4.11 Hvergelmir and primordial rivers

Niflheim, was a realm characterized by mist and frost. In this place was the source of Hvergelmir, an ancestral well from which all rivers were born before they began their journey. The names of these eleven primordial rivers: Fjǫrm, Gunnþrá, Svǫl, Fimbulþul, Slidr, Sylgr, Gjǫll Ylgr, Leiptr Víð and Hríð. From this well sprang all the streams that flowed in the underworld, the earth and the heavens.

It is said that Hvergelmir was fed by droplets of frost that flowed from the horns of Eikþyrnir, a sacred deer. This sacred beast, which was located inside Valhalla, fed on the leaves of the Léraðr tree.

Some of the rivers that flowed out of Hvergelmir even reached the sky so as to reach the abodes of the gods.

Others, however, were the rivers that flowed through the world of humans to the world of the nonliving.

The Slidr was a river that came from the east through the poisoned moors. Swords, blades and daggers floated in these murky waters.

From the dripping slime of the legendary wolf Fenrir originated the River Van. The hideous beast had its jaws wide open as an embedded blade prevented it from clamping them shut, thus leaking out all the nefarious slime that gave rise to the stream in question.

The most famous of the hellish rivers was the Vaðgelmir, feared by the unsuspecting and untruthful since legend has it that once they died they would have to swim in it for the rest of eternity.

Other important rivers to mention are the Kǫrmt, the Qrmt, and the two Kerlaugar. Thor to travel to the assemblies of the gods was forced to pass over them every day since, as mentioned earlier, he could not use the Bifrost Bridge, which would burst into flames when his legendary chariot passed.

Among the cosmic rivers, one of the most important was the Ifing, which divided the realm of the gods from that of the giants. Odin claimed that the waters of this river were sacred, that they never froze and would continue to flow until the night of time. This river was of fundamental and strategic importance for the balance of the nine worlds; it prevented opposing forces, eternally at war with each other, from meeting.

Scholars, in fact, think that the Ifing and Uthaf rivers are nothing more than the same river, but with different names.

Chapter 5

Scandinavian deities

As we have seen in previous chapters, the Æsir lived in the center of the cosmos and their kingdom was called Ásaheimr. In these magnificent lands, on the tops of their highest mountains, the gods founded their stupendous capital called Asgard, full of fantastic buildings and temples, going there to live with their families. From the heights of that place, as magnificent as it was difficult to reach, the Æsir controlled the world, establishing their dominion over all the elements and beings on the planet.

As for the Vanir lineage, however, we know very little. We know with absolute certainty where the Æsir lineage settled but not that of the Vanir. Some scholars claim that their kingdom was west of Ásaheimr, but this is only a hypothesis. We do not know their lineage; we do not know from whom they came or who their leader was. Their kingdom was a very remote land called Vanaheimr. It is thought that they were a people with supernatural powers, with great expertise in magical arts. Vanir women were the main custodians of such arts. Their peculiarity was that they could predict the future. They were a very closed and hostile society, and the practice of incest was very common. Not infrequently, in fact, intermarriage could be witnessed.

According to the transcripts of some scholars, it is thought that in the past between the two peoples, Æsir and Vanir, there was a bloody battle that ended in an armistice. This armistice consisted, in fact, of an exchange of hostages; on the one hand, powerful lords of Asgard settled in Vanaheimr and on the other, powerful Vanir sorcerers settled in Asgard.

The Scandinavian Pantheon consisted of fourteen gods and goddesses charged with ruling Asgard. There were no differences in power and reverence between female and male deities.

Standing out among all these deities was the ruler and lord of Asgard, Odin. Ruling the fortress, just one step below Odin were all the others: Bragi, Baldr, Thor, Freyr, Njǫrðr, Týr, Váli, Heimdallr, Höder, Vidarr, Ullr and Loki and Forseti.

The female deities, on the other hand, consisted of: Freyja, Lofn, Gefjun, Gná, Frigg, Sága, Snotra, Eir, Fulla, Vár, Vǫr, Syn, Hlín and Sjǫfn.

Odin, the wisest among the Æsir deities was nicknamed Allfǫðr, literally the "father of all," since he was the progenitor of all gods. Although all Asgardian deities had equal power, Odin was the most feared and respected as the progenitor and ruler of all things in the world. His wife was the goddess Frigg.

Odin had many sons, prominent among them in strength and impetuosity was the thunder god Thor. Thor was born of incest between Odin and his daughter Jǫrð. The thunder god was the strongest of the living creatures in Asgard. Later Thor took Sif, nicknamed the woman with the golden braids, as his wife; they had two children, a son named Móði, and a daughter, named Þrúðr. But they were not the only children of the thunder god. Thor, in fact, had another son, had with the giantess Járnsaxa, named Ullr. The latter was famous for his skills as an archer and skier.

Odin had another son, also from Frigg, named Baldr. Baldr stood out for his beauty, wisdom and kindness. Indeed, he was considered the best among all Æsir, and was loved and respected by all. Baldr's wife was Nanna, daughter of the powerful Nepr. The two had a son, Forseti, who was considered the judge of the deities. Baldr's brothers were the blind god Höder, and the speedy Hermóðr.

Odin had so many sons and was the father of so many other deities. Another of these sons of his was Vidarr, whom he had with the giantess Gríðr. Vidarr, after the thunder god Thor, was considered the strongest of the Asgardian deities. Other sons of Odin were Váli (had with the princess Rindr) and the fearless Týr (although many scholars claim that the latter was actually the son of the giant Hymir).

Other important Asgardian deities include: Bragi, famous for his eloquence and skill in poems and skaldic arts. His bride was named Iðunn, and she was the one who guarded the sacred apples that the gods used to eat to prevent aging by remaining so young and strong. Let us also not forget Heimdallr, the guardian of Asgard, who was raised by a group of nine young mothers, all sisters. And last but not least, we must mention the god of deception Loki, adopted son of Odin.

Concerning the other divine lineage, the Vanir, as we said earlier, we have very little information. We do not know where they came from, nor do we know who their ruler was. Of this divine lineage, as opposed to the Asgardians, we know only the names of those who moved to Asgard as hostages, who would have shared divine rank and dwelling place with the Æsir.

The names of these Vanir taken hostage, after the war between the two divine lineages, were Njǫrðr and his children Freyr and Freyja; offspring the latter had from his sister. However, incest between such close blood relatives was not permitted among the Æsir.

Upon reaching Asgard, Njǫrðr and his sons, one by one, joined in marriage with local people. Njǫrðr was the first to be united in marriage; he married the fearless daughter of the giant Þjazi, Skaði, also nicknamed Skaði the Fair. Theirs, however, was not a happy and prosperous marriage. Later to be united in marriage was Freyr, who joined the dazzling Gerðr , eldest daughter of Gymir. So good was the good for Gerðr that Freyr unhesitatingly gave up his legendary sword (we will go into this in more detail a few chapters later). And finally came the turn of Freyja who took Odr as her husband, who, however, could not be considered a perfect husband since he neglected his wife by being away from home all the time.

Soon after came a comely and seductive woman Vanir who sowed discord among the gods, corrupting their minds and morality. The name of this Vanir witch was Gullveig. Gullveig was an expert witch in sowing hatred and discord; sowing hatred, envy and greed was her bread and butter. She was even able to corrupt even the minds of the goddesses who had hitherto been guardians of morality and honor. Since the problems with this witch were not about to end, the Æsir decided, therefore, to sentence her to death. The Vanir opposed this choice, calling for her immediate return to Vanaheimr.

Odin knew that not heeding this warning would inevitably lead to confrontation. Nevertheless, the sorceress's attitude absolutely had to be punished. The Asgardian deities erected a funeral pyre, binding the sorceress to it and setting her on fire. Only on the third attempt did Gullveig's body catch fire. The death of their countrywoman was the cause that triggered the wrath of the Vanir, deciding, thus, to declare war on the Æsir.

The two lineages fought incessantly, resulting in a very bloody and violent battle. The struggle between the two factions remained in constant balance, demonstrating the extreme valor of both sides. At one point the Vanir, using their powerful magical arts, managed to breach the mighty walls of Asgard. The battle, however, was now in its last throes; the two factions were exhausted. The Æsir therefore decided to sign an armistice, a truce with the Vanir by exchanging hostages who would respectively live in Asgard and Vanaheimr . The Asgardians gave Mimir and Hoenir as hostages to the Vanir, who in turn handed over Njǫrðr, his son Freyr and daughter Freyja.

As a sign of peace, to seal the newfound serenity between the two peoples, emissaries of both races brought a ram's skin on which they spat as a sign of reconciliation. From the skin of this ram was born Kvasir, the wisest being in the entire cosmos and a striking testimony to the agreement made between the two divine races.

But the already tenuous truce between the two peoples was immediately tested by the people of Vanaheimr. The Vanir, used to seek advice from the learned Hoenir, the latter, however, liked to dispense advice only after confronting Mimir. The Vanir, who were certainly not known for their patience and decided, therefore, to behead Mimir, as they were tired of always having to wait for the confrontation between the two Asgardians to get the answers they sought. As soon as Odin learned of this he flew with his horse to the realm of the Vanir, and filled with hatred, grief and contempt, he had the head of the decapitated Asgardian deity handed over to him, filled it with magical herbs, thus stopping its decomposition process and preserving its wisdom. It was from that time on that Odin while still availing himself of Mimir's wisdom often asked for advice on what to do to the decapitated Asgardian sage's head.

Chapter 6

Asgard: The realm of the gods

The heavenly realm, home of the Æsir, was considered a sacred land. This realm, dotted with ancestral rivers, was extremely difficult to reach unless one knew the right runes that allowed passage along the magical rainbow bridge Bifrost. The roots of the sacred ash tree Yggdrasil reached all the way to the heavenly realm where the sacred spring of Urdarbrunnr was also located.

This heavenly realm did not have a specific name. Humans used to call it Goðheimr, literally "realm of the gods," but according to some scholars its real name was "Ásaheimr realm, or "realm of the Æsir."

At the center of this sacred realm was the rock of Agard. It was there that the main temples and buildings of the Æsir could be found. Also on that rock, not far from the main temples, was the hall of Valhalla. The fate of the twelve ancestral kingdoms depended on this mythological rock. Such was its relevance to the gods that they decided to build their dwellings on it as well

Following the completion of Asgard, Borr's sons (Vili, Vé and Odin) were responsible for the construction of Valhalla.

Initially, the Asgardian fortress was protected by a wooden fence, but after the rupture caused by the war against the Vanir, the gods decided to build the fortress enclosure with very high and impregnable stone walls. This was how the mythical Asgardian fortress came to life. Because of the impregnability of their walls, the gods decided to go and live there with their families, as it represented a safe and inaccessible place.

Right in the center of Asgard was the great vortex, where the deities first gathered in the mists of time to begin the construction of the fortress. Also at that place, according to the historian Voluspá, all the Asgardian deities would meet again later at Ragnarök.

The gateway to Asgard was called Ásgrind. The first building in Asgard was Glaðsheimr. Inside Glaðsheimr were the twelve seats of all the deities, plus Odin's sacred throne. This fantastic as well as majestic and primeval Asgardian building was all covered with gold both inside and out. It was considered by far the most beautiful building in all of Asgard.

Also in Asgard we could find (as we mentioned earlier) the hall of Valhalla, where the great ruler Odin received the Einherjars.

Instead, the shrine of the Goddesses was called: Einherjar. Actually not all scholars agree with this name; for many the real name was: Gimlé. It is said that Gimlé was a palace destined not to succumb even before the devastating flames of Ragnarök and would later become a stupendous and glittering home for all the righteous men who lived throughout history.

Just as in Glaðsheimr Odin's throne dominated the twelve seats of the Æsir, so Asgard was surrounded by twelve ancestral worlds in which the deities raised their marvelous homes.

Himinbjǫrg, the "mountain of heaven," was the fortress that stood at the edge of all creation, the place from which the Bifrǫst bridge came to life. As mentioned earlier guarding the Bifrost was the dreaded guardian Heimdallr, whose job was to prevent the giants from climbing to the mountain walls that led to Asgard. Loki claimed that the life of the guardian Heimdallr was not at all exciting being always on the alert and on guard; the only thing capable of brightening his days, entirely devoted to the defense of the Bifrost was some good mjǫðr (an Asgardian drink).

Odin built for himself a fortress called Valaskjálf, literally "fortress of the fallen." To pay homage to Odin's construction, the other deities covered the latter with living silver. In that sacred building stood the Hliðskjálf throne. Odin's throne had primarily a strategic function; it allowed him to see everything that was happening in the nine worlds by simply sitting. Because of the location of his throne, Odin was able to understand and witness everything that was happening in the nine worlds.

But it was not only the Æsir who lived in the heavens; the Álfheimr clear elves also lived in the heavens, not far from the realm of the Irsir.

Fólkvangr, literally the "people's field," was Freyja's realm and was given to her as a gift from all the deities for her first tooth. Also in that place was Sessrúmnir, (place of spacious benches). The reason for this name was quickly stated; Freyja would choose her diners, who died in battle, from time to time based on the ardor and courage they showed in war. In fact, half of the Einherjar belonged to her, while the other half belonged to Odin.

The thunder god Thor, on the other hand, lived with his entire family in a place called Þrúðvangar, "field of strength," or rúðheimr, "house of strength." In that place he had built a majestic residence, Bilskírnir, "thunder of light." Among the roofed buildings ever constructed in asgard, Thor's abode, after Valhalla was the largest ever built. The fantastic as well as monumental edifice had six hundred and forty rooms and was full of stupendous arches. It was here that good Thor, god of thunder, used to rest after exhausting battles.

Ullr, however, built his own court called Ýdalir, that is, the "valley of the yew." In that place as mystical as it was evocative, Thor's stepson skied over snowy mountains in search of animals to hunt with his mighty bow.

Another stupendous heavenly abode was Søkkvabekkr, also called: the building with "submerged benches." This abode belonged to Sága and stood on cold, icy waves. Odin often joined Saga in his palace to drink and bivouac together.

Baldr's dwelling was called Breiðablik, literally "ample splendor." Baldr built this abode to make his wife Nanna happy. The abode built by the latter stood on a place so sacred that it did not have a single evil rune within it.

Forseti's dwelling was called Glitnir, called the "most glittering" among the houses of the gods; here Forseti established his court. The roof was supported by imposing columns of gold and entirely covered with silver. Anyone who entered to find peace after various conflicts emerged invigorated.

The house of Njǫrðr, called Nóatún, the "fortress of ships," was famous for its imposing temples. It was erected on the seashore. So close was its proximity to the coast that one could hear the swarming of seagulls in the early morning and the ubiquitous smell of seaweed. It was regarded by all the deities as the abode of perpetual serenity.

Also to be counted among the divine kingdoms is Þrymheimr, the fortress of the giant Þjazi, erected among the peaks of

Jotunheim. Following the death of its lowest ruler, it was in fact inherited by the eldest daughter, Skaði, the radiant wife of Njǫrðr.

And then there was Fensalir, the "swamp hall," where Frigg lived with his beautiful handmaids.

Finally, there was a land without a name. It had a dense thicket, full of bushes and tall grasses. There were no buildings, temples or dwellings of any kind. The ruler of that impassable and nameless place was Vidarr, who had lived in those woods since he was a child. The latter spent his days riding majestic colts.

Chapter 7

The afterlife: Valhalla and Hel

As mentioned earlier Valhalla was a huge hall located in Asgard. Only the most deserving warriors could feast within it. The task of accompanying these virtuous warriors into the magnificent palace was entrusted to the Valkyries. The other half, the unawares, the less deserving warriors, would never pass through the gates of Valhalla; only those of Fólkvangr, the camp of the goddess Freyja, would open for them.

The moment the warriors donned their armor, their only thought was about Valhalla and reaching that place. Accessing it was their one and only thought. They were able to fight fear simply by thinking about what would await them after death. Thus, even the fear of dying was no longer a limitation for these valiant warriors; they knew that if they lost their lives in battle in the most virtuous way they could, they would have their place secured in Valhalla. This magnificent palace was supported by beams made from the affiliated spears of the most virtuous and daring warriors. The ceiling, on the other hand, was covered with gleaming gold shields, skillfully decorated with battle scenes. The interior part of the building was furnished with the soldiers' clothes.

In the center of the huge room a giant flame was burning. On either side of this room were two very long benches. There was always room for newcomers, and food was served by the Valkyries in abundance. The huge table was set with all kinds of delicacies; beer and mead were poured continuously into the goblets of the warriors.

As we mentioned earlier, only the most deserving, daring, and courageous warriors, also referred to as "champions," could feast in Valhalla. There were many gates leading into Valhalla, and each of them could accommodate a capacity of about eight hundred warriors. Entering Valhalla was considered a real feast. Waiting for the warriors at the entrance to each of these legendary gates were jugglers who delighted in acrobatic games with swords and daggers covered in gold.

However, not all gates to Valhalla were the same. To the west, in fact, was the main gate where only warriors chosen by Odin himself could pass through; its name was Valgrind. The Valgrid was a majestic gate closed tightly by a magical formula. In order to pass through this gateway, the chosen ones, had to swim across the Thund River, infamous for its danger. Guarding the mythical gate were two sacred figures of Norse mythology: a voracious wolf (representing the ferocity of war) and an eagle (another sacred animal in Scandinavian mythology). Inside this palace, intended for "champions," was a very large courtyard that could accommodate all the warriors who had died in the countless battles that had broken out since the dawn of time.

Once the banquet was over, the heroes flocked to the benches, which, carefully covered with straw, allowed them to sleep until the golden rooster crowed.

The next morning, in the grip of an irrepressible urge to fight, the heroes brandished their weapons and fought without any fear, with the sole purpose of increasingly deserving a rightful place in Valhalla.

They were anything but mock battles. The Vikings loved to fight, and they did it like madmen. The champions did not do it just for the sake of killing; their goal was to train for the divine battle that would take place at the end of time. Together with Odin, the daredevil warriors would fight against the Muspelheim dwellers. Once the fighting inside the huge camp was over, the valiant warriors would gather up the pieces of their bodies and, as if nothing had happened, pass through the gates of Valhalla to merrily feast.

Other very important figures, which it is only right to count, were the Valkyries, whose job was to choose those who died in battle to be "ferried" to Valhalla. These legendary warriors, were female demigods, armed with spears and shields. Indestructible and immortal, Valkyries galloped through the air during wars, never leaving Odin alone, ready to take the souls of virtuous fighters. In Valhalla, on the other hand, these indomitable amazons poured frothy beer and delicious mead to champions.

All these heroes were fed by the cook Andhrímnir, who daily cooked the sacred pig Sæhrímnir, endowed with the incredible power to be reborn each time at dawn, only to be cooked again in Eldhrímnir's pot.

In addition to beers, the heroes sipped a drink called mead. This drink flowed in abundance from the udders of a giant sacred goat named Heidrun located on the roof of Valhalla. The supreme Odin, on the other hand, was the only one who drank wine specially prepared just for him. Odin's throne was located in the northernmost part of Valhalla. Odin often sat on that throne during celebrations of his heroes and was always accompanied by his four sons, Týr, Hod, Vidar, and Vali, all gods of war.

As mentioned earlier, not all warriors were worthy of entering Valhalla. The liars, the fighters who were guilty of grave faults, the creeps and the slothful had an afterlife entirely dedicated to them: the realm of Hel, daughter of the god of deception Loki. This queen of the realm of the dead had two faces: one half normal, the other half cadaverous. Her abode was a very gloomy and ghostly edifice, had no comforts of any kind and was situated in the opposite direction from the sun. Hel's realm was completely different from Valhalla; we could say that it was exactly the opposite. There was no abundance in its dishes and no festive atmosphere in its realm. The main dish for the warriors who went there was famine, starvation and pestilence.

Of all the nine worlds, Hel's was surely the most inhospitable, perpetually stormed by icy winds, thick fog and torrential rain. Even light could not enter that desert of wasteland and despair.

The entrance to this narrow and terrifying realm was a dark and very deep cave manned by a fearsome and ravenous monster called Garm. This hideous beast with half-human, half-beastly features had an insatiable appetite and fed on the blood of the unsuspecting warriors who plummeted into Hel's realm.

The road leading these warriors to Garm's cave was impassable and full of obstacles. Before they could gain access to it, however, along their way they would encounter a giantess ready to examine them. The reason for this precaution was simple: to prevent access to those who were there only out of curiosity about the afterlife. Subsequently to this bridge they would finally come before Queen Hel's gate, a symbol of entry to the afterlife but also of no return.

Just before entering inside, placed before the gates of the afterlife, there was a rooster whose task was to wake up the hordes of unsuspecting warriors who had fallen asleep waiting to cross the pass. Specifically, the rooster's task was to wake them up to pit them against the gods and men who resided in Valhalla in battle. The song of this infamous rooster was chilling and powerful enough to be heard throughout the afterlife.

Somewhat like Dante's circles, the realm of Hel, was divided into various environments according to the punishment or torment that was inflicted.

For example, in the Naigrindr region, the condemned were prodded incessantly by a huge giant and forced by hideous female-looking beings (as opposed to Valkyries) to drink goat urine (as opposed to the mead that flowed from the udders of the sacred goat on the roof of Valhalla).

The beach, on the other hand, was called "death beach." Murderers, adulterers and perjurers who were continually bitten by dragons and extremely poisonous snakes ended up here. To get to this beach, the dead were forced to cross a river filled to the brim with knives, daggers and razor-sharp blades and swords.

On this nefarious beach, an ever-working shipyard was manned by monsters whose job it was to pull the fingernails off their victims. The air at this shipyard was unbreathable because of the stench caused by the excrement that covered the beach. The construction site was always working because the condemned men had to complete the Naglfar vessel made only of nails. This terrifying ship was supposed to transport Hel and her children to Valhalla for the final battle against Odin and his cohorts once Ragnarok arrived.

Also in that place, on an island in the middle of the sea, was exiled Fenrir, the giant wolf who was Odin's arch-enemy.

Chapter 8

The Principal Male Deities

8.1 Odin: the progenitor of all gods

Odin, son of the giants Borr and Bestla, was the eldest of the Æsir. Born in the mists of time, together with his brothers Vili and Vé, he was primarily responsible for the creation of the entire universe and the slaying of the giant Ymir. From the giant's carcass he forged the earth and sky, created the reckoning of time, and established a new world order no longer dominated by giants but by deities

Since Odin was the father of all deities and all things in creation he was served and revered by all the gods. The respect he enjoyed was not because of his strength (the other deities were also very powerful) but because of what he represented, namely, a father to be protected and loved. In fact, he was called Allfǫðr, "father of all," for he was the father of all men and all deities, creator of everything that through his power he brought to fruition.

Odin's kingdom was Asgard and his home the silver palace Valaskjálf, called the "fortress of the elect," which housed not only the ruler of the gods but also all his children and grandchildren. It was Odin himself who erected such a building. His throne, the Hliðskjálf, was located there and served Odin to scrutinize and understand what was happening in the nine realms.

Frigg, his bride, was the daughter of Fjǫrgynn, and she had two sons by Odin: Baldr and probably also the blind Höder. As mentioned earlier Odin did not have only two sons; he had many and by many wives. Thor the thunder god was his favorite son as well as the strongest of his sons (actually in terms of raw, naked physical strength, without the powers derived from Mjolnir, Thor's brother Týr was stronger). Thor was born from the union of Odin and Jǫrð, another of his countless wives. Thor not only had many wives, he also had many mistresses, and among them was Rindr, who bore him his son Váli. Another famous mistress of Odin was the giantess Gríðr, who gave birth to Vidarr, also referred to as the "Silent One." Hermóðr was also considered Odin's son. To the list must be added, the fearless Týr although many think he was the son of the giant Hymir.

Odin also had many sons by ordinary mortals. Many of these sons later became kings or great heroes.

There were so many names by which Odin was known in the human world. There were so many that few were aware of the totality of the appellations. It is thought that, initially, he had twelve names. In order they were Biflindi Allfǫðr, Jálkr, Herjan, Viðrir, Hnikarr, Sviðurr, Óski, Hnikuðr, Fjǫlnir, and Ómi.

He was, as well, called Sigfǫðr and Valfǫðr since he decided who should triumph or perish in war. Odin was also called the "deity of the hanged, and the "deity of the affections."

One reason Odin had so many appellations was because there were so many languages and peoples in the world, and each of them prayed to Odin with their own idioms.

Always hooded, Odin roamed the nine realms on the back of the best steed in all of Asgard: his horse Sleipnir, who had not four but as many as eight legs. He was also accompanied by two wolves: Freki, the "glutton," and Geri, the "devourer," who ate the food on his own table. It is said that Odin did not need any kind of food or drink other than wine. He ate only wine, specially prepared only to meet his needs. No one drank the same wine as the ruler of the gods.

Perched on Odin's shoulders were two ravens who whispered to him whatever they saw or heard. Their names were Huginn and Muninn, "thought" and "memory." They, would fly all over the kingdom and at the end of the day, would return and tell Odin everything so that Odin could get an idea. For this reason another of his nicknames was, Hrafnaguð, "lord of ravens."

One cannot speak of Odin without mentioning his wisdom and the exaggerated knowledge he possessed, for he was the longest-lived and oldest of the gods and creator of all things.

It was he in the first place who learned all the arts so that he could pass them on to the world of men as well. Among the various appellations given to the ruler of the gods, many referred to his immense wisdom and knowledge: Fjǫlnir and Fjǫlsviðr, "very wise," Sanngetall "the one who knows the truth," Saðr "the one who tells no lies," and, again, Forni, "the longest-lived," meaning knower of all things.

Odin's wisdom had no limits: he knew the beginning of everything, the mysteries of the nine kingdoms, all the races of living creatures, but one of his best peculiarities was to predict the future. He was able to foretell the future and knew the fate of every man and all the beings who lived in each realm, but also what was yet to happen. He was aware of the fate of every man and the entire universe.

Odin loved to compete against wise and strong beings. In disguise, that of Gágnraðr, he risked his life by challenging Vafþrúðnir: a very wise giant, known and appreciated in each of the nine realms. However, following a multitude of questions and queries about the future of the nine worlds posed Gágnraðr , the giant Vafþrúðnir answered all but the last one correctly, thus decreeing his defeat. Toward the end of the challenge, Gágnraðr had recognized Odin but by then it was too late.

Odin's challenges, in disguise, were not over. He made another one by revealing himself as Gestumblindi. Odin competed against a ruler named Heiðrekr. The competition involved a challenge of riddles and trick questions. After a few questions that the ruler was able to answer without any reticence, Odin decided to pose the same pitfall to him that he had previously posed to Vafþrúðnir, but the ruler was able to recognize Odin and therefore attempted to stab him. However, he did not succeed in the feat of killing the father of the gods, as Odin transformed into a raven and managed to fly away, escaping.

Odin had always drawn wisdom and knowledge from Mimir's head, which he always carried with him. For him it was an inexhaustible source of inspiration; it was Mimir, together with the two ravens, in fact, who revealed to him all that was happening in the other worlds and advised them how to act.

As mentioned earlier, Odin had only one eye, because one he had pawned off to tap into Mímisbrunnr's fountain of wisdom. From this mutilation come the epithets "eye of fire" and "one-eyed"

The real origin of Odin's wisdom, was another and absolutely not insignificant: he knew every secret and could read and interpret the runes. -Since this is not the subject, we cannot dwell too much on what runes are and what significance they have in Norse mythology; basically we can say that runes are nothing more than engravings on stone, typical of Norse and Celtic culture, in general of the barbarian and northern peoples, which tell the origin of everything and give those who read them infinite wisdom and knowledge.- Explaining how the father of the gods succeeded in such a feat(that of gaining eternal wisdom) is he, Odin, himself, who in this excerpt explains exactly how he came into possession of his boundless knowledge:

"Here, I am aware, I hung on the tall wind-dampened trunk for nine whole nights, struck dead by a spear. On that ash tree that no one knows from what roots it springs. I was very hungry but no one was there to give me a piece of bread; I was thirsty but no one would give me a mug full of water. I looked down at the bottom, screaming with all my might, raised the runes and then fell from there!"

In this way, Odin was able to obtain the magical runes by gaining all his powers. Odin immediately began to feel stronger, reborn, but most importantly, he felt alive!

It seemed that the ash tree on which Odin hung was most likely the huge ash tree Yggdrasill, from which he derived the appellation "Yggr's steed," in memory of his sacrifice.

It was the sighs of Ygdrassil that warned Odin of the prophecies of Ragnarök. He was absolutely aware that Surtr would sooner or later lead the giants in their war against the gods and put everything to the sword. Odin knew full well that he could not prevent this end, but in his heart, he hoped he could save something of the world of gods and men. He could not prevent the end altogether; Ragnarök was a judgment, a terrible truth that could not be avoided.

Thus, Odin, disguised as a gray-bearded old man, headed over the Bifrǫst rainbow bridge to Midgard and began to search for Mimir's well of wisdom. The well was located in the roots of Ygdrassil in Jotunheim. It was guarded by Mimir, the one who drew necessary wisdom and knowledge from the well every morning by drinking a mug from it. Mimir also watched over the sacred horn called Gjallar, which Heimdallr, the white guardian, would blow on the day of Ragnarök.

Odin traveled for many days, meeting men and giants, challenging and being challenged. Once he discovered where the well was and, too, the enormous price he had to pay to tap into its knowledge, he decided to accept the pledge demanded by Mimir. He sacrificed one of his eyes and obtained the knowledge and wisdom needed to rule the nine worlds

Mimir took his Gjallar horn, filled it to the brim with water from the holy well and gave it to Odin.

Odin took the horn and drank deeply. His eyes were opened and he saw the great and horrible sufferings that would befall both men and gods: the Ragnarök.

He drank twice and saw the ways in which gods and men-with nobility of spirit-fought and defeated evils. He also saw his and Fenrir's end. He observed, even, how Thor would die at the hands of Jörmungandr and his poison and how Loki would fight tenaciously against Heimdall. He also saw his own death, at the hands of Fenrir, and many other deaths that would happen at the hands of Ragnarök.

After seeing each of these things, Odin, with his hand over his face, vehemently plucked out his right eye, Mimir took it and threw it into the sacred well in such a way that anyone would be aware of the price Odin had to pay for his knowledge.

Afterwards, he returned to Asgard on his throne, taking into account what he had seen.

Odin's wisdom was pure knowledge, magic and poetry. It was not only erudition for its own sake but also the source of his strength. He was able to put his arts into action with runes or magical songs, also called "galdrar." For this reason the Æsir were also remembered as the "craftsmen of songs." But there were songs-which in all probability were not within the reach of everyone-that only Odin knew and that gave him immense power and luster. Nine of the most powerful spells and magics were learned and handed down to Odin by his maternal uncle, the son of Bǫlþorn.

With his magics, Odin knew how to unite the soul and will of men. These spells were able to quench hatred and diatribe, curb anxiety and sadness, and even heal sickness. On the other hand, the ruler of Asgard, knew how to bring misfortune, sickness and death to men. He knew how to take away the knowledge or power of one man and give it to another. These kinds of spells, which Odin knew very well, were called "seiðr." Outside of Odin, it was the priestesses who practiced these spells since it was considered deplorable for a man to resort to such stratagems.

Odin knew very well how to seduce a woman by stirring love in their hearts; not even the most cunning girl was able to resist him. Odin spoke thus of himself, "I know this: if I wished to have the love of a woman, however cunning she might be, I would bend the girl's candid arms making her forget any thought of her, intoxicating her with flattering words."

If the fire was burning brightly, Odin knew what words to use to quell it. If there was a stormy sea, Odin calmed the wind and waves according to his will. One day I affirmed, "If ever fire should burn the banquet where my heroes who are celebrating, there would be no flame so blazing as to prevent me from extinguishing it through my powerful spells, and I would add, moreover, that if ever my heroes were in trouble with the stormy sea I would be able to stop the waves and calm the waters through my powerful spells."

Odin could not, in any way, be bound or imprisoned. He was able to change form so as not to be recognized so as to conceal his true identity. Odin also used to transform himself into a seagull, fish or snake. It is these three, the sacred animals for Odin. Another sacred animal for Odin was the raven; he could go anywhere, no matter the distance, in the blink of an eye he would arrive back in Asgard to take care of his royal business.

Odin knew where all the riches of the nine worlds were hidden. He was able to raise the dead from the underworld, or to sit by the gallows and loosen the tongues of those sentenced to death by hanging who reported their knowledge to him. For this reason Odin was called the ruler of spirits, the dead and the hanged. In fact, he once stated, "If I saw a man hanging on an ash tree, high above, I would engrave and paint runes in such a way that the man would walk with me and answer my questions."

If Odin saw witches flying in the night, he knew what to do to confuse and dispel them

A great many nicknames were given to him to celebrate his sorcerer skills: Ginnarr, "the trickster," Glapsviðr, "he who was able to enchant," Gapþrosnir, "the sorcerer," Gǫndlir, "he who possesses magical abilities," Haptaguð, "the god of bonds," Skollvaldr, "the strong god in deception," and Svipall, "the shape-shifter." Odin was able to pass on most of his skills to his followers, who together with him learned about the magical arts. However, as time went on, other deities also learned many spells and magics thus giving rise to new magical practices that spread throughout the Nordic countries spreading like wildfire.

Odin claimed that he always spoke in metaphors. It is also thought that he himself started the art of poetry in northern Europe.

The father of the gods was, as we know, the father of poetry. Poetry, in Norse mythology, was considered on par with the magical arts. Odin was able to take from Suttungr, a giant, the sacred mead drink that made poets of those who sipped it. From then on he was the one who guarded it. It is said, too, that the king of the gods gave what was left over of that mead to the world, thus granting men the immeasurable gift of song.

Odin was considered the main deity of battles. He was referred to as Sigfǫðr, "father of all victory," since he decided to whom victory in war should go, and Valfǫðr, "father of the chosen few," since all the children of Asgardian women were his adopted sons. Through these two appellations, Odin distributed victory and death in battle-both gifts highly prized by valiant warriors.

Other names by which Odin was referred to were Fráríðr, "(he who) rides fearlessly to (battle)," Gǫllnir, "(he who) lives in the din," Atriðr, "(he who) proceeds on horseback," all epithets that led back to this warmongering aspect of his.

The father of the gods possessed an infallible spear forged and given as a gift by the dwarves, its name was: Gungnir. On the tip of this sacred spear were engraved runes. With the help of this weapon, he started the first war between two powerful lineages: the Vanir and the Æsir. From then on, before every battle, he turned it toward the host to whom he had sentenced defeat. He was, in fact, also called Dresvarpr, "the one who defends himself with the spear," Geirloðnir, "the one who points with the spear," and Biflindi, or "the one who shakes the tip of the staff." Odin even possessed a golden breastplate, so that he was called Hjálmberi, "he who wears the breastplate."

Odin instilled a certain fear of enemies because of his terribly authoritative appearance. His ability to change form in battle as needed, moreover, only heightened that fear. In battle, he was able to blind, deafen, or terrify his opponents to death, to unleash terror in their eyes, to render any weapon useless against him, and to wound enemies as easily as men were able to snap a twig. He was practically invincible and his opponents were aware of this, which is precisely why they feared and respected him.

No one could throw a spear, in the melee, so hard that Odin could not stop it with a single glance. His warrior skills had a background of magic, for they derived from the runes and the knowledge of them by which he could cast spells and magic. "I am sure," Odin told Loddfáfnir, "that if I had absolute urgency to chain my enemies, thanks to my magical powers I could control their daggers, their shields and even their swords."

On the other hand, he himself chose who to protect and who not to protect in the fray of battle, so as to protect and make untouchable his favorite heroes. Odin could make sure that those who went into battle would not suffer a single scratch and would come out safe and sound. One day he asserted decisively, "If I must lead my valiant warriors into battle, I will sing under their shields, so that they may emerge victorious, safe and sound."

It was Odin who determined the fate of the heroes. He gave them victory and decided when, where and how they should die. The heroes were devoted to Odin and trusted him with their eyes closed and invoked him as Sigfǫðr, "father of all victory," Sigtýr, "God of all victory," Sigþrór, "bring luck in battle," Sigðir, "servant of all victories," Sigtryggr, "faithful in wars and successes," Sigrhǫfunðr, "prince of triumphs," and "Sigmundr," protector of triumphs."

Achieving success in battle or dying gloriously were two things of equal importance to the Vikings. Posing this question to a warrior of Odin could only lead to a neutral answer; indeed, many preferred a glorious death to an unsuspecting victory. In fact, the fate of those who perished in war in clashes was far from grim. Those who fell in battle were considered true "chosen ones" by Odin. Odin welcomed them as his adopted sons and brought them to the hall of Valhalla, where they participate in the eternal banquet headed by himself. Odin was therefore also known as Valfor, "progenitor of the elect," Valtyr, "deity of the dead in battle," Valbognir, "the one who welcomed the dead in battle," and so on. At one time, Odin manifested himself, to a seer resurrected from beyond the grave, as the first-born son of Valtamr, which stood for "accustomed to choose the best fallen in battle," also in fact this was one of his innumerable appellations.

This is how Odin chose the champions who would later accompany him in the final battle of Ragnarök. These heroes would form the ranks of the Einherjar: a cohort of spirits who would ride the skies alongside the supreme Odin on stormy nights. The father of the gods was also known as Hertyr, or "God of the cohorts."

The congregations of ecstatic warriors were linked to the cult of Odin, the berserkers and úlfheðnar, also referred to as "the bear-clad" the former, and "werewolves" the latter. Before each war, these types of fighters would catapult themselves into a state of fury and excitement, referred to as "berserkers," in which they would begin snarling, drooling, and biting the ends of their shields. Afterwards they would throw themselves, screaming at the top of their lungs, into battle, drawing swords and wielding mighty axes, making scorched earth all around them. These mythical warriors felt neither pain nor fatigue.

With a hat on his head and a cloak on his shoulders, often wielding his spear as a simple staff, Odin roamed the roads of the nine kingdoms. In fact, he was also called Vegtamr, " the wayfarer," or Gagnráðr, "he who knows every road," and again Kjalarr, "he who uses a sled."

Odin roamed the streets of the nine kingdoms as a poor beggar, concealing his true appearance and real identity. For this reason, he was also called Grímnir, "he who wears a mask," or Hǫttr, "the hooded beggar," and again Lǫndungr "he who wears a cloak," or Hrani, "the jibbler." He was usually shown as a wise and elderly man with a very long and full beard because of which he was called Harbarðr, or "grizzled beard," Langbarðr, "full beard," Síðgrani, "the well-groomed," Sioskeggr, "he who had a fine beard," and Hengikeptr, "the man with wrinkled cheeks."

Odin was, in fact, the god of travelers and those who headed anywhere. During his long journeys, he asked for shelter for the night, both in the homes of the rich and in those of poor and humble people. He was also referred to as Gestr, "the guest." In fact, any wayfarer hosted could be Odin incognito. Hospitality was sacred to the Vikings mainly for this reason. You never know whether or not your guest may or may not be the ruler of the gods himself: Odin.

Once, in the disguise of Grímnir, Odin was received as a guest by the ruler Geirrøðr, who, suspicious, mercilessly tortured him, imprisoning him between two flames that never ceased to burn. Having revealed some of the most mysterious secrets of the divine world and others concerning some of its most famous epithets, Odin finally revealed himself. The ruler Geirrøðr immediately ran to free him but tripped his sword and fell on it and died pierced.

For this reason, the supreme Odin took the names of: Jálkr when he was hosted by the people of Ásmundr; Gagnráðr when he competed with the giant regarding topics dealing with remote knowledge; and many others all related to the experiences and vicissitudes he experienced.

To be honest, he was a very large and wise man who knew each of these stories about him with certainty.

The appearances of the supreme Odin were a topic dear to Norse traditions. Indeed, Scandinavian myths document many accounts of men encountering along various paths a beggar, an eerie-looking traveler, who sometimes introduced himself by one name rather than another. He would often knock on the doors of various houses, hoping for hospitality for the night. Those who had to deal with this particular beggar understood that he was not actually a real traveler, and only at the time of his departure, sometimes days later, did they realize that they had met the mighty Odin.

Often Odin meddled in the lives of kings and legendary warriors, bringing them into existence, giving them help on several occasions, and even decreeing their deaths if necessary. To corroborate this thesis we can report the history of the Vǫlsungar lineage, which was thought to derive directly from Odin himself and which the god himself convincingly protected for many generations, until legendary warriors were born from that lineage; among them we can count Sigurd, Sinfjǫtli, Helgi and Sigmundr.

So many were the circumstances in which Odin took their side, giving them a helping hand and wise counsel. However, at the right opportunity, he would claim their souls. One day, in fact, Odin showed up to demand, by right, the body of Sinfjǫtli , thus removing it from his arms and from the funerary boat, and it was he again who personally provided the spear with which Dagr could finish Helgi.

This was only one among many examples we could cite. In another context, for example, Odin revealed himself, in the guise of Hǫttr, "the hooded one," before the presence of the comely Geirhildr and arranged for her to become the companion of the ruler Alrekr. Later, he gave the woman a hand in brewing good beer because of a competition by asking her what stood between her and the pot-he was referring to the child she held in her womb. Víkarr, then, the son, was born already consecrated to the God Odin, who made him a sublime warrior and a great king.

But then, as told in another legend, Odin returned as Hrosshársgrani, "the man with a mustache who rode a horse," demanding the death of young Víkarr, a boy whom, years earlier, he had blessed. A false hanging was staged. It was hoped that this "clowning" would satiate Odin's thirst for death, but inadvertently, the mock hanging turned into a real sacrifice and Víkarr perished, with a noose around his neck and pierced by Odin's spear.

It is always told in the legends in his honor that the powerful ruler of Denmark Hrólfr Kraki was met on a trip to Norway by a creepy peasant boy named Rani. It is thought that this peasant boy was none other than Odin.

Odin revealed himself, in the guise of Jólfr, to the ruler Oddr; protagonist, the latter, of a particular legend. Odin gave Oddr three arrows, made from magical stones, with which the young warrior was able to slay a powerful demon. However, revelations from the god Odin were recorded even after the conversion of the Scandinavians from pagans to Christians. One legend tells how the crew of a ship one day picked up a very strange man who wore a blue cloak and claimed to be called Rauðgrani. The latter taught the men the worship of paganism and urged them to make sacrifices to the deities.

Finally, a monk became angry by vehemently striking him on the head with a cross. The mysterious individual plunged into the open sea and never returned. Although this myth does not specifically say so, that hooded man was indeed Odin.

Again in false guise, that of Gestr, Odin visited Óláfr Tryggvason, ruler of Norway (995-1000 CE). The god revealed himself in the guise of an old man all hooded who was endowed with enormous knowledge, wisdom and experience and who reported myths and legends from every country in the world. The strange old man had a very long discussion with the ruler. Afterwards, when it was late at night, he left. The next morning, the king of Norway looked for him but the old man had already disappeared by then. Before he went, however, he had left a huge amount of food for the banquet of the ruler Olaf. At this point Olaf, a fervent Christian, ordered that the food not be eaten, for he understood that the old man was none other than Odin in disguise.

In the same guise as Gestr, Odin revealed himself again a few years later before King Óláfr II of Haraldsson, known as "the Holy One." He appeared before the ruler's court in the guise of a proud and scurvy man. He had a wide-brimmed headdress that covered his face and a very thick and long beard. During the conversation between the two, Gestr described to Óláfr the image of an old-time king who was so wise as to express himself through the use of poems and rhymes. The latter excelled in every battle and could grant victory to others as well as himself as long as he was invoked. From these words, Óláfr quickly realized that what he had before him was Odin and drove him away.

8.2 The god Bragi

Among the Æsir there was a deity called Bragi. He was one of Odin's sons and possessed enormous wisdom and knowledge. Some of the most powerful runes were engraved on his tongue, and this was, perhaps, the reason why he had a very sharp tongue and not inconsiderable oratorical skills. Even better was he at the lovely art of poetry, of which he even proclaimed himself the creator. From his name descended the skaldic art also called "bragr"; the man or woman who was able to possess at the highest level total mastery of the art of oratory was recognized as "bragi." Bragi had a long, thick beard, and knew every kenningar and all the poetic metaphors by heart, which he taught to Irgir at a banquet, without concealing from him the sagas and legends from which they originated.

Bragi's bride was named Iðunn, and she was the goddess who guarded the apples of eternal youth. Bragi had both blood children and adopted children.

He was certainly not known for his warrior skills. Bragi, while appearing proud and fierce when necessary, claimed to be ready to fight with anyone if it was needed, but he preferred to calm tempers rather than stage silly battles. He always preferred dialogue to confrontation. When Loki insulted him, in Irgir's court, calling him a poor coward, he preferred to calm the situation by giving him as a gift a filly, an axe and a necklace; but, since the other had no intention of ceasing in provoking him, Bragi stymiedly stated, without half-measures, that he would behead him if only they were not in Irgir's presence.

On the other hand, although not a warrior, Bragi assiduously frequented Valhalla, where, together with Hermóðr, he welcomed the most distinguished rulers who died in battle.

8.3 The god of deception: Loki

Loki was a pivotal figure in the development of many Norse sagas. The cunning god responsible for chaos, deceit, pitfalls and double-crosses, rather than an actual deity, was the materialization made in person of fraudulent cunning and the subtle art of deception.

A solitary man, Loki was a cryptic individual for several reasons. The etymology of his name comes from fire. This is a singular aspect in that fire is, yes, an element interconnected with the development of societies, but it also represents the antithesis of construction that is, destruction. Loki, we could argue, is this: creation and destruction at the same time. Although he was an Æsir, he was originally part of the lineage of ice giants, who represent chaos and destruction; in fact, he was often referred to as the "shame of the Æsir." Loki was a true professional liar with only the desire to annihilate under the radar the order assigned to him. In some sagas he was the faithful companion of Odin and the thunder god Thor; if they were able to overcome certain challenges it was precisely because of Loki's cunning.

Loki, therefore, was not known as an evil deity in the strict sense. He helped both the gods and the giants according to the course of action most congenial and advantageous to him in that particular circumstance. He embraced both Asgardian and giant values. His presence was, therefore, vitally important so that the two compartments, that of the gods and that of the giants would remain in balance with each other. Loki unabashedly represented the needle of the scales in a feud that had lasted since the dawn of time.

Loki had somatic traits of rare beauty that, at the same time, inspired admiration but also instilled awe; all of which was a clear indication equivocality distinguished him. He was the eldest son of the giant Farbauti, also called the "merciless attack," and the giantess Laufey, also called the "marvelous island." The two giants had a secret alliance with Odin by giving Loki into his care as a sign of submission.

The sexuality of the god of deception was quite fluid. He was famous for giving birth to an offspring of ruthless creatures whose purpose was the end of the world and the destruction of everything. It can be argued that sons of Loki were far more evil than their father. But not all beings born of Loki were evil. For example, Odin's mighty and swift steed was named Sleipnir, and she was one of the beings born of Loki's will.

Angrbodha, his daughter, was the giant prostitute who was condemned to the stake for her misdeeds. Loki was an extremely sadistic deity. In proof of this theory it is said that when the body of his daughter Angrbodha was reduced to a pile of ashes the god of deception watched the scene ecstatically, reached down, took her still-living and beating heart and devoured it in one gulp. The hate-filled heart of the giantess, impregnated Loki, who later gave birth to three lowly beings: a wolf-like beast, another snake-like beast and a little girl. All three beasts grew up in Jotunheim so that Odin would not discover their existence. Noting how dangerous they were, Odin commanded that they be brought before him so that he could decide how to render them harmless by neutralizing them. The descendants of the god of deception, as mentioned earlier, would prove to be far more terrible and evil than the god of deception himself.

The wolf was named Fenrir. At first, the deities decided to keep him in the gardens of Asgaard; however, the fearsome beast came to grow out of all proportion. He grew not only in stature but also in intelligence and ferocity; only Tyr, fearless and mighty brother of Thor dared to feed him. Unfortunately, the ravenous and gigantic wolf became too much of a danger and all the Asgardian deities made the decision to imprison him. Fenrir would remain chained until the coming of Ragnarök; when he would be set free and could take revenge by feeding on the body of the king of the gods, Odin.

The snake, on the other hand, was exiled to the depths of the deepest seas, where it grew to a mammoth size. Its coils became so thick and strong that it was able to envelop the entire world in a single vise. It, too, would rise from the depths during the Ragnarök, annihilating all of humanity with its very powerful bite. He will later die, confronted by the god of thunder, Thor. However, Odin's son will also die soon after, poisoned by the bite of the giant serpent.

The girl, on the other hand, a symbol of despair and famine was Hel, ruler of the underworld. Her appearance was gruesome, at times vomiting. Somewhere between a rotting corpse and a human being. Hel was taken into exile to the farthest reaches of the earth and in those very places crowned, by the deities, queen of the underworld. Hel unlike Fenrir and the serpent had no grudge against the gods, as they had made her queen and ruler of a kingdom. It was for this reason that she gave Odin as a gift two ravens Huginn and Muninn who served as her advisors. Odin, therefore, entrusted her with the task of imposing the torments and punishments to be inflicted on anyone who was not chosen to enter Valhalla. Hel became the ruler of the honorless fallen, traitors, cowards, and murderers and liars.

Loki was given a terrible punishment for causing the end of the god Baldr. He was taken to a dark cave in Niflheim where the deities decided to turn one of his sons into a ravenous beast that in turn fed on another of the god of deception's sons. Thanks to the entrails of the mauled son, the gods were able to bind Loki to a huge boulder where the poisonous slime of a snake, placed in the air by the deities, dripped incessantly onto his face. This venom was so strong that it caused Loki to feel a continuous burning sensation. The screams and cries of the king of deception were so loud and charged with pain that they generated tremendous and violent earthquakes in all the nine worlds.

Loki must remain in this state until the day of Ragnarök, when he manages to free himself by siding with the ranks of evil alongside his progenitors, the ghaccio giants. He will clash with the guardian of the rainbow bridge, Heimdall, in a fight to the death that will see them both perish in battle.

8.4 The mighty god of thunder: Thor

Thor, was the eldest son of Odin and his wife Jòrdh, an earthbound deity. He was the lord of gales, storms, and thunder and protector of the sacred city Asgard; ceaselessly involved in destroying ice giants and conducting legendary deeds. Such peculiarities led Thor, in the collective imagination, to be represented similarly to Tacitus' Hercules.

The thunder god was a deadly, sensational fighter, the most feared among the Æsir; he possessed three main weapons: metal sleeves, a girdle that disproportionately increased his powers, and the world-famous Mjölnir, the sacred hammer capable of turning back once thrown at enemies.

Thor had a very thick, long beard of a deep red color with very long, shaggy hair. His pupils looked like burning flames. His coming was heralded by the rumble of thunder, and his incredible chariot was drawn by two rams-Tanngnjostr and

Tanngrisnir. It is said that at one time, blinded by gluttony, he devoured them both and then brought them back to life simply by resting his mighty Mjölnir on the rams' cadeveri. Farmers idolized him since he was the companion of Sif, deity of abundance; it should also be added that the Mjölnir, symbolized the thunder that anticipated the downfalls, vital for the harvest. The thunder god lived with his wife in Asgard's most majestic palace, the silver palace, but he had many other relationships with both humans and giantesses. In fidelity he had nothing to envy his father Odin.

During Ragnarök, he will fight to the death against the giant serpent son of Loki and emerge victorious but will die shortly thereafter as a result of the venomous bite of the hideous beast.

8.5 Týr

Týr was the eldest son of the ruler of the gods, Odin and his wife Frigg. Considered the deity of knowledge, wars and laws. He was originally the strongest and most powerful deity, a role later assumed in the Scandinavian era by Odin.

He was also the god to whom the strongest fighters turned just before battles, the talisman of every great victory for which protection was sought. He was by no means a deity pro heinous and exasperated confrontation but, rather, the guardian of battles understood as the only possible way. He also represented the god of justice, but not understood as reconciliation but, rather, as confrontation between the parties. Just as in a jury, precisely, the challengers followed an unwritten rulebook by engaging in validating the verdict of the confrontation. The winner represented reason. The winner represented reason, and Tyr wrote the verdict with the blood of the defeated warrior.

Týr, similar to his father, Odin, lost a portion of his body, his right limb to be exact. The enormous wolf Fenrir, the beast son of the devious deity of deception, posed a very large threat to be disregarded by the gods, who decided, therefore, to imprison him in the bowels of Asgard with sturdy sacred chains. Fenrir, however, was too strong, skillful and cunning, and just like his father, Loki, he always had a solution to the problem. In fact, it was because of his memorable cunning that he was able to free himself from the chains that imprisoned him. The king of the gods, Odin, therefore decided, using the ancient magical arts handed down to him by the dwarves, to construct a magical lasso, capable of chaining even the most hideous beast, challenging Fenrir to break free from it. The beast, cunning just like Loki, said yes to the competition but on one condition, namely that a deity would stick a limb into his jaws during his imprisonment. Thor's brother immediately agreed. However, although all attempts by Fenrir to free himself from the sacred lasso that held him bound were in vain, he still managed to bite Tyr's hand. Thus obtaining a small revenge. But, it was thanks to Tyr's sacrifice that the gods managed to chain the hideous wolf to a rock and point a huge sword at him that ripped through his flesh whenever he tried to struggle.

Týr, already a victim of Fenrir, will die in Ragnarok at the hands of the underworld guardian dog Garmr

8.6 Baldr

Baldr was the most beautiful and kind-hearted deity that existed in Asgard. He was the favorite son of Odin and his wife Frigg, and was loved and respected by every living being. He was an example to all gods; his heart was never corrupted by morally deplorable attitudes. Never a word too many or out of place came out of his words. Never arrogant, never boastful and always most modest. These were the peculiarities of Baldr. However, he did not enjoy much sympathy from the other deities. In fact, because of the other gods' envy of him, the advice he bestowed was never taken into consideration.

His mother, Frigg, was aware that Baldr was destined for an untimely death, so she decided to travel throughout the universe in search of a solution. She called every plant, beast and every element in the whole of creation to account, obligating them to a timeless pact: no one and under no circumstances would harm a hair on Baldr's head. The god of deception Loki, as always envious of everyone, especially Baldr, transformed himself into a comely mortal woman in order to be able to talk to Frigg so as to deceive her and ask her what the weaknesses of the pact made by the woman and the elements of creation were.

Loki took mistletoe seedling from the ground as he approached Höder, Baldr's blind relative, who was left alone and aloof. Through one of his usual deceptions, Loki gave

Höder the small mistletoe plant, and as if it were an arrow helped him by taking aim with him. The throw was so accurate that it pierced Baldr's heart, causing his immediate death.

From this legend, we can learn that Baldr represented the embodiment of innocence made in person, misguided, betrayed by the envy of those around us-an utterly pessimistic view of the world that characterizes the entire worldview in Scandinavian culture and art.

The gods tried to have Baldr's soul returned to them by the queen of the underworld, who agreed but on one condition: every living being, living or dead, human or beast would have to weep by showing sincere sorrow for his loss. Only the god of deception Loki, in the guise of an old beggar woman, did not weep, binding Baldr to a fate of suffering in the underworld. In fact, one of the most famous appellations for Bladr was " God of Tears."

8.7 Heimdall, the guardian of the rainbow bridge

Heimdall was the guardian of Asgard and the Bifrǫst rainbow bridge, the famous bridge that connected heaven to earth. The sister of this mythical guardian was named Sif, and she was the wife of the thunder god Thor.

It is not known exactly why Thor had entered into a relationship with Sif. We do know, however, that Heimdallr was the son of nine different mothers and that his father was Odin himself.

We also know of Heimdallr that he was called "the shining warrior" and that he possessed unparalleled strength. He defended the entrances to Asgard many times because of his formidable skills as a soldier and warrior.

He watched over Odin's realm unceasingly, and just like the father of the gods he received great powers by depriving himself of part of his body: he cut off part of his ear and buried it near the roots of Yaggdrasil, receiving unparalleled sight and hearing in return. Thanks to these abilities Heimdall was able to scout out any threat from the universe.

He was the keeper of the magical horn Gjallarhorn, through which he was able to warn the deities whenever Asgard found itself under siege. During Ragnarök, the task of this horn would be to resonate throughout the new worlds to summon the warriors of the two factions that had always been at war with each other: good and evil. Heimdall to his ill degree, will witness the collapse of the Bifrǫst rainbow bridge, destroyed by the relentless forces of evil. She will successfully fight Loki, succeeding in killing him, and sound the horn for the last time, rallying all the forces of good in Asgard. The image of a burning Asgard will remain forever etched in his eyes.

Two creatures that accompany Heimdallr are the golden rooster Gullinkamb, whose job is to wake up Odin's soldiers each morning to incite them to battle, and the golden horse Gultopp.

8.8 Vidarr

Vidar, was the third strongest Æsir, after Tyr and the thunder god Thor. He was the son of the great Odin and the ruthless giantess Gríðr. He lived in Asgard in the peaceful hall Vidi provided with a huge garden. He was known to have been a very taciturn individual at peace with the elements of nature in his garden. The sagas and myths tell that he would stand around all day in his magnificent garden working on a special shoe.

This particular boot made from the discarded and trashed skins in Midgard was the most durable ever produced up to the hour. Vidar will use this special shoe to take revenge, on the day of Ragnarok, for the death of his father by placing it in

Fenrir's jaws, thus breaking his jaw, but failing, however, in his intent to kill the hideous beast.

8.9 Forseti

Forseti, was the son of Nanna and Baldr. Promulgator of laws he was also called "the god of justice." He himself often stood as judge in conflicts between deities. His task was only to enforce the laws. Very often he spent his days meditating and studying.

8.10 Freyr

Freyr, was one of the most beautiful gods in all of Asgard. God of fertility, prosperity, wealth and crops he was a member of the Vanir, and son of Njǫrðr. Freyr had a sister named Freyja and had the giantess Gerðr as his wife. On the day of Ragnarök, Freyr will be forced to pay for this love with his own life.

He often used his chariot, carried by his boar, Gullinbursti, to travel very long distances.

8.11 Hermod

Hermod was the son of Odin and his wife Frigg. When Baldr died, it was he who rode his steed to Hel to try to bring him back from the underworld.

8.12 Njǫrðr

Njǫrðr was the wind god. He was part of the Vanir lineage and was father of Freyja and Freyr. Njǫrðr was married to Skadi, a feared giantess.

8.13 Mimir

Mimir was the god of knowledge and wisdom. During the war between the Æsir and the Vanir, Mimir was driven out by the Vanir. But it was not long before the Vanir searched for him, found him and decided to behead him by sending his head to Asgard in defiance. Odin, in order to preserve Mimir's knowledge, availing himself of the use of his magical arts managed to preserve the head thus preserving his knowledge and wisdom.

Chapter 9

The Principal Female Deities

9.1 Iðunn

Iðunn was the goddess of youth. Iðunn had the exceptional gift of averting death and premature aging for all deities. She was said to have taken this power together with her husband Bragi through special knowledge in the medical field. Bragi was the god of the arts, poetry and advisor to Odin. In fact, in the ages to come, it was claimed that Iðunn's powers were derived from some magical apples of which she herself was the sole cultivator. The goddess, therefore, was responsible for continually supplying these apples to the other gods, who, by eating them consistently, would remain young for eternity. The most famous legend related to Iðunn was her abduction by Þjazi the giant.

Iðunn was depicted as a beautiful woman, looking like a woman in her twenties or even a teenager. She had very long blond curls and always held a basket full of apples.

Bragi, her husband, was depicted as a man with a very full beard, always devoted to playing the harp, a symbol of the arts and poetry.

According to some myths, Iðunn's apples also had the power to instill fertility in those who ate them. For this reason, she was also known as the Scandinavian goddess of fertility, just like the goddesses Freyja and Sif. In fact, Iðunn had some peculiarities in common with these two female deities. Sif had long blond hair, while Freyja was often depicted with flowers in her hair or as a mysterious woodland creature. There are a great number of paintings and illustrations depicting her together with cats, symbols belonging to Freyja but also of the goddess Frigg, Odin's bride.

9.2 Freyja

Freyja was the goddess of love also associated with lust, fertility, sex and battles. She lived on Fólkvangr, the "people's field," and was the daughter of Njǫrðr. She had a twin named Freyr, and was married to the deity Odr. With him she had two sons, Hnoss and Gersemi.

Although she belonged to the Vanir lineage, she had become an honorable member of the Æsir after the end of the feud between Æsir and Vanir.

She was thought to have a beautiful appearance and long blond hair and was usually depicted in rural and country attire. She often wore a dress made of flowers and was surrounded by animals. She represented an object of desire not only among deities but also among giants and dwarves. She loved jewelry and fine materials and often employed her beauty to get what she wanted. She owned a necklace known as Brísingamen.

Freyja loved to travel in her carriage, pulled by two cats. She was also able to fly with her cloak adorned with hawk feathers. Freyja owned a boar named Hildisvini, which she rode when she was not using her carriage.

The union with Odr was said to be very peaceful, although the latter was often away from home, leaving his wife in tears.

Scholars are not sure whether Freya was a faithful companion or not. There are many stories that she was involved in lustful love affairs, such as the one with the god of deception Loki.

9.3 Sif

Sif was the goddess of grain, abundance and crops. She had long, beautiful golden hair and was married to Thor. She had a son named Ullr. One day Loki, while Sif was sleeping, cut off her long hair. But he was later forced by his brother Thor to give it back to her.

9.4 Frigg

Frigg was the chief deity of love, unions, fertility and motherhood. She was the ruler of Asgard and wife of Odin. She and Odin had two sons, Baldr and Höder. She was the stepmother of Bragi, Heimdall, Hermod, Höder, Týr, Vidar, Thor and Vali. Armed with the same knowledge as the god of all creation Odin, Frigg also possessed the gift of foresight, which she used to predict future unions and births. Along with Odin, she was also the patroness of all manual arts and crafts, especially traditionally female arts, such as weaving, which is said to have been passed down personally to all women.

The origin of another of his symbols, the bunch of keys, was not known. Frigg was said to always hold a set of keys in her hand, but the myth explaining its motivation was, with the passage of time, lost. A probable explanation for that legend was that the keys represented the goddess's ability to open all portals to the unknown worlds thus increasing her wisdom and hunger for knowledge.

She was the only deity who was allowed to sit on the sacred throne of the all-powerful Odin, the "the Hlidskjalf." The only throne capable of giving those who sat, a glimpse of the entire known universe.

She had three handmaids named Fulla, Gná and Hlín. The former, always close to her mistress, had the arduous task of serving, caring for and assisting her within the walls of the house. Especially in Frigg's personal estate, the Fensalir. The Fensalir was Frigg's magnificent personal home within Asgard. Hlín had, on the other hand, the task of acting as an ambassador and carrying the Goddess' messages to earth in the guise of a hawk. Gná performed both Fulla's and Hlìn's duties. She was regarded by Frigg as a kind of joker to be counted on in the most critical moments.

Fulla was undoubtedly the most powerful of the three handmaids. She was depicted with very long hair, by the side of the goddess, and always holding a casket. Fulla always held this casket in her hand since one of her most important tasks was to carefully fold Frigg's socks and shoes and then place them in her mistress' casket. Frigg and Fulla are sacred to winter, especially the days immediately following the solstice, during which girls are forbidden to spin as a sign of respect to the queen of the gods. Fulla, besides being a maid, is also Frigg's confidante and keeper of her secrets.

The power of the young Hlín, able to transform into a huge hawk, came from a mythical cloak made of hawk feathers-in all likelihood it was Frigg herself who made it. This particular cloak allowed anyone to fly through the skies of the nine worlds and go unnoticed thanks, precisely, to the transformation into a hawk.

Chapter 10

The Ragnarök: the end of everything

In Scandinavian mythology, Ragnarök represented the event that sanctioned the end of everything, everything. The gods would fight against the giants in a war in which both sides would lose their lives. The last act of the battle between the forces of good and evil had just begun. Preventing The Ragnarök was impossible, and any action taken by the gods to avert it would be utterly vain. Ragnarök was the means by which the rejuvenated and completely purified universe could begin a new ancestral cycle. It was, therefore, the end of one cycle followed by the beginning of a new one; a new creation and a new end continuing thus for eternity. In a nutshell, we could consider Norse mythology as two opposite ends within a circle; at one end a point represented by creation, another by destruction. One cannot reach one end without encountering the other. Destruction and creation are inevitable, inescapable and eternal, as are good and evil

The warning that would herald Ragnarök would be the end of young Baldr; stabbed by the god of deception Loki and forced to remain in the realm of the dead. This forced the deities to face their fate of mortality and not immortality, as they initially thought. Despite their not being human, they were in fact subject to the same fate as any living creature: death exists for the gods as well. However, being aware of it did not lead the gods to a resignation and acceptance of reality. Although all forms of resistance against the fate that awaited them were in vain, the ruler of the gods and all the other deities did not back down and still gathered the strongest and most valiant warriors who would help them in the final and timeless feud against the ice giants.

The second sign was the complete cessation of things as they were known, over all the concept of civilization and order in the society of men. Men will forget their customs, cultures and traditions by disregarding all kinds of kinship, initiating bloody fratricidal feuds and indulging in deep nihilism. Depravity will be the only motivation to drive human beings forward. Fathers will murder their offspring, while mothers will do anything to seduce them. Brothers will have incestuous relationships with sisters, (although the concept of morality and monogamy will come only with the arrival of Christianity, incest was still viewed very deplorably by the Norse).

Next will come a very harsh winter (called Fimbulvetr), which will completely unhinge the summer for more than three years. Frost, gales and terrible torrential rains will make the globe a very inhospitable place by enveloping it in a thick and unbreakable sheet of ice.

The last signal, the third, will be the loss of Sòl, the sun, and Mànì, the moon. The Skoll and Hati beasts, which had been chasing them since the dawn of time, will finally be able to catch up with them and eat them, taking away the light of the sun from the world, thus plunging it into perpetual darkness. Consequently, all the stars will implode and fall down from the celestial vault, causing the sailors to spin wildly in an ocean where light can no longer show the way.

The final battle will begin as soon as the three roosters proclaim the coming of Ragnarök. One rooster, will inform the giants and giantesses in Jotunheim, another the fallen in the realm of Loki's daughter Hel. Warning the gods, however, will be the mythological rooster Víðópnir, perched atop Yggdrasil. The huge ash tree, which contained the nine kingdoms in its mighty branches and roots, will falter, shaking the entire universe with harsh earthquakes that will render the earth a heap of shreds.

At the exact moment when Yaggrasil falters all the chains will break. The god of deception, Loki, and his son Fenrir, the enormous wolf, will manage to break free from the long imprisonment that kept them segregated, thus roaming the nine realms and sowing destruction and despair. The enormous serpent, Jormungandr, also the beast son of Loki, bound in the depths of the seas, will re-emerge from the waters, causing tidal waves, flooding towns and cities with all their inhabitants.

Naglfar, the mighty hellish ship, built in the underworld with the nails of doomed warriors, will rise from the bowels of hell carrying the army of evil, ready to raid.

The mammoth Fenrir will run through the new worlds with his jaws wide open. He will be so large and terrifying that his upper jaw will be able to graze the heavens while his lower jaw will graze the landmasses, annihilating whatever shows itself before him. Jormungandr, the brother beast, the serpent of the new worlds, will fight at his side. The two mythological beasts will destroy everything by spreading hunger, destruction and misery throughout the earth

Led by Surtr, a giant capable of destroying worlds with his fearsome sword of fire, the slimy people of Muspellsheim beginning their advance from the south will reach the Bifrost rainbow bridge, leaving behind their passage infernal streaks of fire that would incinerate anything they encounter.

Unable to resist their passage, the bridge will collapse causing the terror lords to advance toward Asgard. Here the inhabitants of Muspellsheim will meet, with their natural allies: Loki, his sons and all the outcast beasts imprisoned in Asgard, on the plain of Vigrid. The entire evil of all the nine worlds will gather there, in Asgard.

Meanwhile, Heimdall, the mighty guardian and keeper of the rainbow bridge, would run out of Himinbjorg, his huge hall, and call all deities to attention through his horn. This would be a warning to all deities that the final battle had just begun.

Odin, with hate-soaked eyes, fiery red eyes and a heart full of indomitable courage, will wield his fearsome spear, don his mighty helmet and mount his mythological six-legged horse Sleipnir. Arriving in the valley of Vigrid he will gather his best warriors, his strongest sons and all the deadliest Asgardian deities. The Asgardian army will be so numerous that it will turn the entire Vigrid plain into an ocean of swords and shields.

In the eyes of the warriors of Asgard there was no fear or qualms whatsoever. They were proud, serene, and happy to meet their destiny. No fear received. Ragnarok represented the end of everything but at the same time the beginning of everything, where all the gods who represented good would fight against the giants who, on the other hand, represented the forces of evil. The one great desire of the Asgardian warriors was to fight and to do so to the death.

Odin was certain of this. In order to have any more hope he would first have to face the strongest of enemies: Fenrir. The god of thunder, Thor, will not be able to help him because he will fight against the giant serpent Jormungandr. Odin, too sure of victory, will be killed by Fenrir's fearsome jaws. His son Vidar, will see the whole scene and moved by an irrepressible rage will kill the mighty wolf.

He opened the powerful jaws of the hideous beast and, aiming with his feet on the lower jaw, was able to exert such strong pressure that the entire jaw was destroyed on Loki's son. In doing so Vidar was able to avenge his father, but the beginning of the end had just begun.

Freyr , later on, will duel with Surtr but will die for handing over his sword to his slave and fixer, Skirnir.

The thunder god, making his way through the ranks of the giants with the mighty blows of his Mjöllnir, fought against his arch-enemy of all time, Jormungandr, who was so great that he covered the whole of creation. Thor's strength was immense. After a very long and grueling battle he succeeded in crushing the skull of the hideous beast, causing it to sink into the depths of the seas. Thor's strength, however, was only apparent. In fact, after nine steps the thunder god will keel over, poisoned by the mighty serpent's bites. The same fate would befall Týr, who, fighting to his last breath against Hel's hound, would slump to the ground after defeating it.

The last of the duels between great characters in Scandinavian mythology will be between Heimdall and Loki, who will die together as a result of the clash. Before drawing his last breath, Heimdall will blow his horn for the last time, then slump on a burning warfield with the image of Asgard's end etched in his terror-filled eyes. Heimdall will be the last of the Asgardian warriors to die and watch Asgard fall.

Many other deities will die, and Surtr, now undisputed master of the battlefield, will put the Earth to the sword, causing the new kingdoms to fall into an inferno made of perpetual flames. Eventually the nine worlds will cease to exist and merge together, creating a new Ginnungagap and thus decreeing a new beginning of the whole.

The forces of good and evil eventually clashed, and neither emerged victorious. Together they faced each other, both inexorably lost. In Ragnarok there are neither winners nor losers. Both are. The role of Ragnarok was that of a purifier, an equalizer who through fire would reset everything. For to make a new world, one must first destroy the old.

Just before the Ragnarök battle begins, a man named Liftrasir and a woman named Lif will take shelter in the sacred ash tree Yggdrasil, the tree of eternal life. As soon as the battle is over, they will go outside to admire the new creation. Both humans will feed only on dew drops, repopulating the world again and becoming the new creators of a new lineage of humankind.

However, not all the deities will die during Ragnarok: Vidar, the son of Odin who defeated the giant wolf son of Loki, and the descendants of the thunder god, Magni and Modi, who will receive their father's sacred hammer as an inheritance, will manage to save themselves. Baldr and his blind brother, Höder, will also return from the dead.

Thanks to the birth of a new world due to Ragnarök, the myth of the Norse gods will come back into vogue.

The survivors will settle in Idavoll, the lush green plain where Asgard once stood. Together, they will build their fantastic new dwellings there.

The daring fighters who joined the side of the gods during the Ragnarök, who died for an ideal of freedom in the world, will not stop bivouacking on good mead and enjoying themselves in the new home of the gods to be called Gimle.

Meanwhile, near Nastrond, the "shore of the dead," the evil creatures will take refuge in a huge building, without any kind of beauty, where the walls will be formed with the skin and venom of snakes that had not died during the final battle.

Chapter 11

Scandinavian myths and legends

11.1 The Deception of King Gylfi

King Gylfi reigned over all of Svíþjóð. The story goes that he gave a poor woman, as a reward for entertaining him, a small patch of land within his kingdom and four oxen so that she could plow both day and night.

This woman was not just any beggar woman; she was a descendant of the Æsir lineage, and her name was Gefjun. Odin, who also ruled over Danmork at that time, had sent the young woman to Svíþjóð in search of new territories. As soon as Gylfi kept her promise, Gefjun headed north to Jotunheim and bore four children she had by a giant. Once they were born, he turned them into oxen by tying them to the plow. The plow dug so deep and deep that it melted a huge patch of land, which the oxen carried all the way west over the ocean, putting it into a strait. Gefjun called this land Sjóland.

King Gylfi was wise and knew many spells. He was fascinated by the enormous strength of the Æsir and wondered whether this power descended from their nature or was given to them by the deities they so loved and prayed to. For this reason, he began a journey with destination precisely the mythical city of the gods: Asgard. To go unnoticed, he disguised himself as an old beggar.

But the Æsir were much smarter than any human, even a king. They, in fact, had the gift of foresight. They learned of his journey even before he arrived and prepared Sjónhverfingar (outer part of Asgard) to confuse him.

As soon as Gylfi entered the citadel, he noticed a palace so tall that the top could hardly be glimpsed. The ceiling was entirely covered with gold shields set like tiles, just as the poets described the sacred hall of Valhalla. On the edge of the doorway stood a man dabbling in acrobatics with seven daggers, a true juggler. The latter asked Gylfi what his name was. Gylfi said his name was Gangleri and that he had asked for shelter for the night since he had come from far away. He also asked whose huge building that was. The juggler answered him that the huge palace belonged to their ruler. At one point, the juggler motioned for Gylfi to follow him to enter.

As Gylfi passed through the huge gates, an ancient saying came to his mind:

"Every door, before it is passed through, must be spied on. It must be spied on and scrutinized."

Arriving in the skáli, the door closed. Inside was a large crowd: those who were bivouacking, those who were enjoying beer and mead, those who were fighting. King Gylfi looked around. Everything he saw seemed incredible to him.

At the bottom of the skáli could be found three huge thrones, side by side, and on each of them sat a man. Gylfi asked the juggler what their names were. The latter told him that the one in the lowest place was the ruler and his name was Hár, "the high one." The one next to him was named Jafnhár, "equally high," and the one in the highest seat was Þriði, "the third."

Hár asked the newcomer if he had any plans, because if not, he could stay and bivouac and enjoy himself with all the other people inside the hall. The conversation between the three kings and Gylfi continued for hours. Gylfi did nothing but ask anything he could think of about the origin of the worlds and the Norse deities. The three deities even went so far as to tell him about Ragnarok. Gylfi could not believe his eyes. He now had all the answers he was looking for about the Æsir.

But the gods as we said before were smarter than any human, even a king, and they knew that revealing those things to the curious ruler would create great dangers. So, Odin, knowing that Gylfi would not keep to himself all the information he had revealed to him under the false guise of the three kings, decided to make him fall into a deep sleep.

Gylfi woke up in his palace, in his bed, in sweat dripping pajamas as if he had been dreaming for days.

In doing so, the curious ruler Gylfi thought it had been a long dream and never revealed anything Odin told him in disguise for fear of being considered insane.

11.2 The construction of Asgard and the birth of Sleipnir

The myths and legends surrounding the birth of Asgard are many and controversial. One of the most fascinating is undoubtedly the construction of the walls of Asgard in conjunction with the birth of Sleipnir. Following the taking of the citadel by the Vanir, all the deities present in Asgard trembled at the idea of seeing their dwellings looted and destroyed.

A few days after the invaders conquered the citadel Vanir, an old craftsman with a long gray beard and very confident eyes, offered to build a huge wall in defense of Asgard. A wall so tall and so strong that it would defend the city even from the mightiest giants. However, in order to accomplish this very grand project, the old man asked for the Goddess Freyja, the sun and the moon in return.

All the deities gathered an assembly to discuss it.

The old craftsman was part of an ancient enemy lineage in Asgard, the Jotnars. The gods clearly had no desire whatsoever to give Freyja away, relegating her to a life in Jotunheim, nor to deprive themselves of the sun and moon.

After much discussion among themselves, the deities in unison judged the craftsman's proposal to be very attractive, but the required reward was clearly out of their reach. So, the

Æsir told the old man that he would get everything that had been agreed upon if he completed the construction in half the allotted time. He would have to work all winter, and if on the first day of summer any part of the wall remained unfinished he would lose the bet and with it his reward. To make matters worse, the poor craftsman would have to work completely alone, without anyone's help. All the deities, were convinced that under these conditions the craftsman would never make it, thus achieving two birds with one stone: an almost completed wall and the safety of Freyja, Sun and Moon.

The old jotnar agreed, but on one condition: that he could use his magnificent stallion Svaðilføri as a helper. The Æsir were not very convinced, they thought there was some kind of trap, so they consulted among themselves to make an accurate decision. Eventually Loki acted as an intermediary between the two factions, vouching for the old craftsman. At this point the gods agreed. The old man had one last request: to be defended by Thor. Being of the lineage of giants, he had no intention of ending up in a hunt for the god of thunder. Thus, at the end of several oaths and perjuries the Æsir would guarantee the old jotnar's safety.

Thus began the first day of winter and with it the first working day of the old man. In no time at all, the wall of Asgard began to take shape, growing day by day, leaving the gods stunned. All the gods gathered again, worried that they might lose the bet. The gods also knew that they would have to honor their promise; they therefore began to think how they could stop the craftsman who, if he continued at that pace, would be finished before the beginning of summer. At that point Odin summoned Loki, intimating that he must resolve the situation immediately or they would imprison him. Loki would certainly have preferred the old craftsman to win the challenge (he loved to sow discord and dissension among people, especially among the gods) but by nature he was also selfish and therefore helped the gods not to lose the bet.

Winter was coming to an end, and the craftsman was traveling expeditiously toward the realization of his dream. At one point, one night before completion, when there were only a few boulders left, the old man's stallion, who had helped him up to that point by carrying heavy boulders, saw a filly in the bushes and chased her, abandoning him with only a few hours to go before the end of the bet. That mysterious filly was none other than Loki, in disguise, with the aim of making the old craftsman lose. In fact, the old man failed to complete the task by going on a rampage. He became filled with the typical anger of giants and tried to attack Odin and all the other deities who were present that first summer morning. At that point Thor, god of thunder and hunter of giants, arrived, whirling his huge hammer whirling down from the heavens, striking him in the face with such vehemence that it broke his skull, sending him back to where he had come from.

That night the two horses chased each other incessantly, never stopping. Tired just before dawn they collapsed together. The stallion upon reaching the filly impregnated her. The filly, who was none other than Loki in disguise, gave birth to Sleipnir, the legendary six-legged stallion, chosen steed of the mighty Odin.

11.3 The children of the god of deception, Loki: the underworld queen Hel, the huge serpent Jormungandr, the mighty wolf Fenrir, and the hand of Týr

Once a giantess lived in Jotunheim; her name was Angrboða. The god of deception glimpsed her heart, toasted in the ashes, and ate part of it. In doing so he magically became pregnant with the giantess and gave birth to three hideous beasts. The first beast to be birthed by Loki was the wolf Fenrir. The second was the huge serpent Jormungandr. The third, a young maiden who had half a rosy and healthy face, the other half bruised and bluish in color. The name of this girl was Hel.

As soon as the Æsir learned of these three hideous beasts raised in Jotunheim, they announced prophecies of misfortune and misery traceable to the birth of Loki's three sons. It was clear that such slimy and terrible progeny would throw Asgard into chaos given their nature but especially that of their father.

At that puto Odin decided to send the strongest gods of Asgard in search of these three hideous beasts in the Jotunheim to catch them and make them as harmless as possible. First, the gods descended into the Jotunheim , captured the huge serpent and threw it into the uthaf, the outer ocean that surrounded all the kingdoms. However, the icy waters of the uthaf had an anabolic effect on the hideous beast, which grew so large that it surrounded the entire world. The serpent ended up encircling the entire globe and finding itself in front of its own tail, it squeezed it in its jaws, encircling the lands in a huge living circle. From then on it took the name Miðgarðsormr, the "Midgard serpent."

Next Odin took care of Loki's daughter Hel. He sent her to Niflheimr and allowed her to build her ghastly palace. He bestowed magical powers on her, making her the goddess of the dead, especially of those who died of old age and sickness, but also of warriors who died unvaliantly.

As for Fenrir, prophecies stated that he was destined to cause enormous misfortune and suffering in the future, and that he would be the one to kill Odin on the day of Ragnarok. The Asgardian deities , however, did not feel like killing the wolf and decided to raise him in Asgard.

As he grew up, Fenrir became increasingly large, fierce, and dangerous enough that no one could approach him; the only one who could was Odin's very powerful son Tyr. --As mentioned earlier, it is thought that Tyr, in terms of physical strength, was the strongest of the gods of Asgard-It was Odin's son in fact who tended the hideous beast by always feeding him alone.

The gods created a very powerful, almost indestructible chain, which they called Løðingr. Once the chain was created they needed a stratagem to chain the hideous wolf. They showed, therefore, the chain to the wolf by offering him a challenge. The Æsir were very clever, but Fenrir was by no means inferior. They asked him if he could break it. Fenrir agreed and had himself tied up. Subsequently, with a very slight pressure he managed to break Løðingr, freeing himself from it nimbly.

But the gods did not give up. They created another chain, stronger than the previous one. They decided to call it Drómi. They came to Fenrir again and asked him to try the challenge again, but this time with a different chain. To convince him, they told him that if he could break it, given the far greater strength of the first chain, he would gain great fame and honors.

Fenrir watched her for a while trying to scrutinize her as much as possible. He quickly realized that the chain was far stronger than the first one, but he decided to meet the challenge anyway; he knew that fame can only come from arduous and dangerous trials. He decided, therefore, to allow himself to be chained. He began to kick and flail so much that he shattered this second chain as well.

Disheartened, the Æsir believed that nothing could stop Fenrir. But Odin still had hope of succeeding in the feat of imprisoning Fenrir. He therefore decided to ask for help from the best craftsmen of all the nine kingdoms, the dwarves. He sent Skírnir, Freyr's messenger, down to Svartálfaheimr, to the land of the dwarves. They gave the Asgardian messenger a lace called Gleipnir. It was very thin, silky, and to the eye also very faint. It certainly did not resemble a large steel chain. The dwarves told the young messenger that this particular lace was made of six things that combined to create the softest but at the same time strongest material in all the nine realms. The materials that made it up were six: the sound of a jumping cat, the beard of a woman, the roots of a rock, the sinews of a female bear, the breath of a fish, and the milk of a bird. This is the reason why from that time women no longer had facial hair, the cat's leap made no noise whatsoever, and roots no longer grew under rocks.

When the Gleipnir lace was delivered to the Æsir, they thanked the valiant messenger for his service and set out in search of Fenrir to offer him yet another challenge.

Once the hideous beast was found, the gods proposed the unusual challenge to the wolf: he would have to get rid of the lace that was so fragile in appearance. Fenrir immediately smelled the deception, but the hubris of one who thinks he has no weaknesses was at an all-time high after destroying the previous chains he decided, therefore, to accept certain of victory. However, Fenrir also had a proposal and before accepting, he proposed a modification to the challenge. He asked the gods for someone of them to put their hand inside his jaws for the duration of the wager. From the Æsir, Tyr was chosen. The challenge began and the more the wolf moved the more this lace tightened on him. Within minutes he found himself completely immobilized by the Gleipnir. The gods had won, but at a price: Tyr's hand, during Fenrir's frantic motions to free himself, had been severed by the jaws of the hideous beast.

As soon as the Asgardians realized that the hideous beast was totally hunted down they took one end of the sacred lace that held him pinned down and tied him to a huge boulder, using the gigantic stone as a peg. Thus they threw the wolf into the earth, and to inflict even more suffering they pointed a huge sword between its jaws that forced it to hold its jaw open.

From that moment, Fenrir began to howl incessantly, and from his mouth gushed out a revolting substance, a mixture of slime and blood, which flowing away formed the river Vàn. He would remain in this condition until the coming of Ragnarök.

11.4 Thor vs. the giant Geirrøðr

There was a time when, Loki, who loved to fly over the Jotunheim, often wearing a suit that resembled the likeness of Frigg's hawk, landed at Geirrøðargarðar, the fortress where the jǫtunn Geirrøðr lived. He descended to a skylight to observe what was taking place inside the hall. Geirrøðr noticed him immediately and commanded one of his servants to capture him and bring him to him at once. However, the skylight was very high, and Geirrøðr's servant could not reach it easily. Loki, who enjoyed seeing others drowning in their difficulties and problems, mischievously stayed there until the last moment. He took great pleasure in seeing the man's efforts to reach him and decided, mischievously, not to fly away until the last moment; he would run away as soon as Geirrøðr's servant finished climbing.

But Loki sinned in presumption, and was so convinced that the clumsy servant would never catch him that he ran away very late. It was for this reason that the man managed in extremis to grab a leg of the bird, catching it and pruning it before the ruler. Geirrøðr looked carefully into the hawk's eyes and the doubt came to him that the bird was nothing but a mutated being. Thus, the ruler intimated to the hawk to reveal its true identity, but Loki did not breathe a word.

Geirrøðr decided, therefore, to test the shifter's endurance and locked him in a box without food for three long months.

When the three months had passed, he let Loki out of the box and ordered him to reveal himself. This time the god of deception did not let him repeat himself a second time and revealed his true identity. To have his life saved, he promised the ruler that he would have Thor arrive completely unarmed; without belt or hammer.

Loki did not put much effort into convincing Thor to go down into Jotunheim to destroy Geirrøðr. The thunder god was always happy to kill some slimy jotnar. However, we do not know Loki's ploy to convince the thunder god to undertake such a risky mission in Jotunheim without his best weapons.

Once they left, Thor and his helper spent the night in the giant Gríðr's dwelling. Gríðr was Oðinn's mistress and mother of Vidarr the Silent.

Being aware of the reason for the journey, Gríðr told him everything he knew about Geirrøðr. He affirmed that Geirrøðr was very wise, grumpy and mangy. He was very difficult to deal with. And since the Thunder God had no weapons with him, he gave him his magic belt, and the iron gloves he possessed. And with them, he also gave him his staff, the Gríðarvǫlr.

After the night had passed and they left Gríðr's house, Thor reached the icy and fearsome waters of the river Vimur. It was the largest waterway in the nine kingdoms. Thor entered the cold waters and advanced along with his helper. Many claim that Loki himself was there, clinging to the belt of the megingjarðar. Others, however, believe it was Þjálfi, clinging to the thunder god's shield belt.

Cold, violent waves crashed against the thunder god and his helper as rocks collapsed under his mighty footsteps. Thor went forward fearlessly, harried and full of indefatigable energy. As he reached the center of the raging river, the waves were so high that they crashed over the mighty shoulders of the thunder god. Next, Thor noticed among the rocks Gjálp, one of the daughters of the ruler Geirrøðr, straddling the two banks of the river Vimur. She was the reason why the waters of the Vimur River were so violent. Through her spells she was able to create tidal waves but only against Asgardian citizens. Thor, who certainly was not one who liked to stand by and watch, took a large stone and with pinpoint accuracy struck the ruler's daughter who was standing on the other side of the river. These were his words, "To dam a river one must first stop the source."

Upon reaching the shore, Thor clung to a wild rowan tree, thus managing to get out of the water. This is the reason why the wild rowan tree is also known as "Thor's helper."

Having crossed the entire river, Thor finally arrived in the Jotunheim, with Þjálfi firmly attached to his belt.

The hearts of the two valiant leaders did not tremble even when they saw before them a very long line of giants waiting for them armed to the teeth

The Jotnar, to intimidate them, began to draw their swords, slamming them vehemently against the shields. The noise caused by the swords, rattling against the shields, was definitely terrifying. But the thunder god was very strong, even without his favorite weapons. He succeeded , therefore, in putting them to flight, forcing them to retreat. Thus Thor, was able to reach as far as Geirrøðr's abode.

There, Thor and Þjálfi arrived at Geirrøðargarðar and entered the royal palace, proud and fearless of the feat accomplished. This their hubris put the Jotnars in great agitation. However, the hideous giants took courage by leading Thor, reluctant to a possible armistice, to the quarters prepared for him: the goat stable.

Inside the room there was only one chair; the thunder god saw it and sat down without blinking. All of a sudden the chair rose, carrying Thor up to the ceiling.

Hidden beneath it were Gjálp and Greip, Geirrøðr's other two daughters, who were intent on crushing the god's skull against the mighty rafters of the roof. However, Thor, pointing

Gríðarvǫlr's rod against the ceiling, made a pressure opposite to that exerted by the ruler's two daughters and came back down. There was a huge commotion, followed by a violent scream. The scream was caused by the king's daughters Gjálp and Greip were crushed under the chair with all their bones broken.

Afterwards Geirrøðr called Thor into the main hall, asking him if he would like to play with him. Huge hearths were arranged along each wall of the hall. When Thor stood before Geirrøðr, the latter took metal tongs set to warm in the embers and threw them at him with extreme force and vehemence. Thor, being much stronger and more cunning than the ruler stopped them thanks to Gríðr's metal gloves, blocked the tongs and sent them back to the sender. Immediately, Geirrøðr took cover behind a pillar. However, the glowing iron went past the column piercing the giant's abdomen.

Filled with wrath and with hearts filled with hatred at seeing their ruler killed, the Jotnars declared war on the thunder god Thor.

Thor killed them one by one, thanks in part to the support of his faithful helper Þjálfi. Thus it was that Thor defeated Geirrøðr and his hateful subjects.

11.5 Thor, the stolen hammer and Freyja's unexpected marriage

One freezing night, while sound asleep, Thor was robbed of his invincible hammer. His deadly weapon was stolen from him by a giant named Þrymr. The next morning once he woke up, Thor immediately realized that someone had stolen his very powerful hammer going, thus, into a rage. He decided, therefore, to talk to his half-brother Loki who, thanks to his cunning and cunning, was the only person who could help him out. Loki began at once. Together with Thor, he made his way to Freyja to ask to borrow her famous falcon disguise. The young goddess was happy to help him and gladly handed it over. In this way, passing unnoticed, the god of deception Loki flew over Asgard arriving as far as the land of giants: the Jötunheimr. Mrymr, while combing the mane of his horse, saw Loki coming and asked him, "Loki...what are you doing here? didn't you live among the Æsir? Why are you here in the Jötunheimr?"

"There is some skirmishing between Æsir and elves," Loki asserted.

"Did you take Thor's hammer? Tell me the truth!"

Mrymr said without hesitation that it was he who had taken Thor's precious hammer, and that he had hidden it in the deepest bowels of the earth. Without equal hesitation, Mrymr stated that he would reveal the exact location of the hammer only if they gave him Freyja in marriage.

At this point, the god of deception returned toward Asgard, to the garden of the gods, where Thor was waiting for him. Before revealing to him what he had discovered, he warmly invited him to sit down. Once he revealed what the giant Mrymr had told him, Thor was shaken but still agreed to go to Freyja. So the god of thunder and the god of deception headed to Freyja and proposed to her that they be united in marriage with the giant. Freyja became very angry going on a rampage, so much so that she caused a violent earthquake that shook all the buildings of Asgard. Such was the wrath of the Goddess that from her bosom broke off the most precious Brísingamen necklace. She affirmed, "Are you so sure as to think that I have such an unbridled lust for men that I would go and marry a giant in the Jötunheimr!"

How can you blame her.

Thus, all the deities gathered in council to find a solution; it was imperative to take back Thor's invincible hammer. The best advice came from Heimdallr, one of the purest of the Æsir deities, who was also famous for his ability to foretell the future, just like the Vanir. Heimdallr ruled bluntly, "Let us dress Thor in a wedding garment, adorn him with the gorgeous Brísingamen necklace. Then, we will place a small bunch of keys at his hips and make a very long dress in such a way as to cover his hairy knees! Finally, we will reproduce his breasts with large stones and comb his untamed hair."

This advice seemed to Thor the best solution to solve the problem. "All the gods of Asgard will call me mad," asserting that if he dressed as a bride he would be mocked forever.

Loki said, "If you don't hurry up and get the hammer, there will be no more Asgardian gods to mock you, only stupid giants around Asgard."

This sentence stirred something in Thor's soul, and he immediately wanted to start with the plan to recover his irreplaceable hammer.

Thus began the preparations, and Thor was dressed and adorned to perfection. He wore Freyja's necklace, a long dress that covered his hairy knees, and his hair had been straightened so well that it looked like string. After that, they moved on to the prosperous breasts reproduced with large stones. Having finished the preparations, Loki stated, "Now we are ready to go into action, I will be your handmaiden and take you into the Jötunheimr."

So together they set out for Jötunheimr on the chariot of the thunder god pulled by goats. The chariot went so fast that every time it passed, powerful shock waves were unleashed that shattered the mountains, and the wheels given the speed with which they turned left scorched earth as they passed.

Mrymr, the king of giants, was ready to welcome the woman he had so longed for until then. He affirmed, "Come on, hurry up! Everything must be ready! In my life I have never lacked anything: gold, jewelry and reverence! The only thing I lack is a bride; I want Freyja."

In the evening a huge table was set up and the giants were served rivers of beer. Thor was terribly hungry and very voraciously devoured a cow and nine salmon. He even drank four barrels of mead. Mrymr could not believe his eyes and began to doubt, and in exhilaration stated, "Have you ever seen a woman drink and eat like a man?"

Loki, who was disguised as Freyja's escort and bridesmaid hastened to explain, "Freyja was very hungry, she had not touched food for days, such was her desire to reach Jötunheimr as soon as possible."

Mrymr was convinced; but, at one point, he came up to kiss the bride and noticed that "Freyja's" eyes were an unusual fiery red, and said, "Why are Freyja's pupils so fiery? There seems to be living flames within them."

At this point the maid (Loki) again took the ball and stated, "His eyes are so fiery and red because he has not slept for days such was the excitement of arriving here in the Jötunheimr."

At that very moment, the ruler's sister entered the room demanding a gift, and asked Thor, "Strip off all the gold rings on you and give them to me if you want my benevolence in return."

Then Mrymr took the floor and said, "Bring that stupid Asgardian's hammer and give it to my sister; this will be her wedding present."

The god of thunder, Thor was waiting for nothing more and once he grabbed his formidable hammer he hit the ruler of the giants so hard that he killed him with a single blow. Thor did not even spare the ruler's sister and killed all the giants present at the wedding feast. Thus, instead of gold and jewels Mrymr's sister found a sound hammering in the face and the ruler a painful death instead of a loving bride. When the slaughter was over, Odin's son took the hammer and flew to Asgard, swearing to himself that he would never again leave his legendary hammer unattended.

11.6 Thor vs. Hrungnir

It is said that at one time, while the Thunder God was in the east killing trolls, Odin headed, with his faithful steed, Sleipnir toward Jotunheim.

Arriving in the cold, icy lands of the giants, an individual named Hrungnir came to him. This giant was enraptured by Odin's phenomenal steed, capable of galloping through both air and sea. He decided, therefore, to ask the identity of the man who, with such skill, rode him. Odin replied with a statement, "There is no better horse in all of Jotunheim than this one."

"Yours, without a shadow of a doubt is indeed a very good horse," affirmed Hrungnir,-"but mine is better, and his name is Gullfaxi, the steed with the golden mane.

He jumped on Gullfaxi's back and galloped following Odin's wake, determined to change his challenger's mind. But Odin's horse galloped so fast that it managed to outrun Gullfaxi and Hrungnir. The giant was so focused on winning that he did not realize he had passed through the gates of Asgard and arrived before the fortress of the Æsir

Arriving at the gates of Valhalla, the gods invited him to drink. He was, therefore, given jugs full of mead; jugs that were usually used by Thor. Hrungnir drank them all, leaving not a drop behind.

Once drunk, the jotnar, he did nothing but boast. He claimed with absolute certainty that he would overthrow the whole of Valhalla, defeat all the gods and bring all Æsir into Jotunheim, while Freyja and Sif would become his slaves. He was certain that he would succeed in razing all of Asgard to the ground.

The Asgardians soon grew tired of Hrungnir's arrogance, and called Thor. The thunder god immediately appeared, holding his deadly hammer, looked around, and rather angrily asked, "Who allowed a dirty, twisted-minded Jotnar to drink with

Asgardians in Valhalla? And why is Freyja serving mead as if we were at a banquet among Æsir?"

Hrungnir looked Thor fixedly in the eye, and arrogantly said, "It was your father, the god Odin, who invited me to feast, and I am under his protection, whether you like it or not."

"A dinner invitation you will soon regret attending!" said Thor.

"You will certainly not be remembered as a memorable warrior if you kill me now that I am unarmed, indeed in all likelihood you will be remembered as a cowardly coward," Hrungnir replied to him, and added, "It was a foolish mistake to leave my shield and hen at home; if they were here with me we could have fought. I am convinced that you must come and fight in the land of giants to give strength to your undertaking."

After that, the jotnar Hrungnir returned to Jotunheim, galloping as fast as he could.

Hrungnir's lightning departure from Asgard made the thunder god very furious. The jotnar had offended him publicly, threatening to kidnap his bride Sif. Moreover, according to the claims of some warriors, it seems that Hrungnir had kidnapped Thor's daughter.

But Thor was not only enraged, he was also very excited. Never before had anyone dared to challenge him to a duel, and this thrilled him. The only thought Thor had in his mind was to get revenge and to do it in the best way possible.

Among the Jotnar the news that one of them had dared to challenge the thunder god Thor ran fast.

The inhabitants of Jotunheim knew that the fate of the two peoples would depend on the victory or defeat of one of the two legendary warriors. The ice giants were sure that they would suffer greatly if Thor killed Hrungnir, for at that point no one else could challenge Thor. Hrungnir was the strongest among the inhabitants of Jotunheim. At this point, the Jotnar molded a man out of clay and placed him on the borders of Jotunheim. He was named Mǫkkurkálfi. They were unable to find a heart large enough, for this clay monster, until they decided to tear one out of a mare. However, the Jotnar were unable to insert it properly into the chest of the clay monster that Thor had already arrived. As for the opponent, Hrungnir, he stood by the clay beast, waiting for his opponent.

His heart, was made of solid boulders and equipped with three sharp horn points, from which originates the symbol called: Hrungnishjartr. His head was also made of boulders, as was his huge, thick shield, which he held before him as he waited for Thor at the edge of Grjótúnagarðar. His weapon was a whetstone, which is a giant stone used for sharpening metals.

Thor wasted no time in chinching , such was his desire for revenge against Hrungnir. He climbed into the chariot pulled by sacred goats and set off. The arrival in Jotunaheim was so mighty and grand that it shook the earth. Even the firmament caught fire, the mountains broke, and the hail that fell from the sky before it touched the ground became pure lava.

Hrungnir, preferred to play smart by relying more on tactics than on strength (he knew, in fact, that a challenge of pure strength would be won by Thor).

Thor's daughter, moved by compassion went to Jotnar suggesting that he put an invisible shield under his feet, otherwise Thor, in order to avoid the main shield placed in front, would go underground and once he popped out would hit him, "Jotnar, you are in danger...if you keep the shield in front. You must know that Thor has noticed it. He will go underground and hit you from below."

Hrungnir willingly accepted the advice of Thor's daughter and placed the invisible shield under his feet, remaining motionless. Matters of moments and amid roaring thunder and lightning Thor made his appearance, who was advancing at an impressive speed. The thunder god with a very powerful hammer blow struck the giant's skull shattering it into a thousand pieces. Then came the turn of the clay giant also shattered into a thousand pieces by his mighty hammer. The two enemies had been defeated without too much difficulty but Thor did not emerge unharmed from the encounter as the clay fragments of the giant struck him, causing him to fall unconscious to the ground.

Thor's daughter tried hard to bring her father to his senses but the father just could not wake up. At one point, Thor's youngest son, little Magni who was a skilled magician managed to wake up his father. The thunder god to thank him gave him as a gift Hrungnir's horse, which was now left without a master. Thus it was that Asgard, in addition to Slepnir had another sacred horse in the stable: the mythical of Gullfaxi.

But once back in Asgard, Thor still had shards of clay in his head that stuck him in bed with excruciating pain. At this point the master of Magni, the chief wizard of Asgard, was called upon: Gróa. This powerful wizard, thanks to one of his spells, was able to expel every shard from Thor's skull, restoring to Thor the strength and vigor he had lost in battle against the two giants.

11.7 How Freyr lost his sword

At one time a man named Gymir had a woman named Aurboða as his wife. They were part of a particular lineage of giants from the mountains. The two had a beautiful daughter named Gerðr.

One day, Freyr was looking at all nine kingdoms sitting on the throne of the almighty Odin. Once he turned northward, he noticed, a huge and beautiful palace. To this building a woman approached.

However, Freyr was severely punished for his insolence in sitting on the sacred throne reserved only for the mighty god Odin. Filled with anger at being reprimanded he momentarily fled Asgard. Once he returned, no one among the Asgardians dared to speak to him.

At this point Njörðr interposed Skyrnir, Freyr's messenger, and enjoined him to head to Freyr to speak and ask him why he was so angry that he would not speak to anyone. Skírnir affirmed that he would do anything to find out why Freyr was not speaking to anyone but he was certain that he would not receive good answers.

Once he arrived at Freyr's, Skyrnir asked him the reason for his sadness. Freyr affirmed that he had seen a beautiful woman and was torn by grief because he would not dare to live one more day without her.

"Skírnir you must set out toward Jotunheim and ask for the hand of this wonderful woman on my behalf. If you complete the mission you will be richly rewarded."

Skírnir answered in the affirmative, coninvinced that he could do it without much effort, but asked Freyr for his legendary sword. The Asgardian thought nothing of it and handed him his sword.

Upon arriving at the mansion of the stupendous woman, Freyr's messenger found large guard dogs at the entrance preventing his passage. Undecided what to do, he turned to a farmer perched on a hill and asked him if there was another entrance to gain access.

"You are already dead, my dear stranger, no one leaves that house alive!"

But, Skirnir was not intimidated by the old farmer. He returned once again to the front of the giantess' dwelling, and once again the dogs began to bark. At that point, annoyed by the constant barking of the guard dogs, the giant Aurboða's servant came out of the house to find out what was going on.

"There is a stranger outside with his horse put out to graze in front of the house."

Aurboða told him to let him go inside and offer him beer.

"My wonderful and enchanting lady," Skírnir exclaimed, "I am here to deliver to you eleven golden apples that can be yours if you claim that there is no more magnificent creature in the nine kingdoms of Freyr."

Aurboða did not accept the golden apples and with them Freyr's attraction and with icy firmness said, "I will never marry Freyr, I will never live with him, and I will never be in love with him."

Skírnir attempted, therefore, to give her as a gift the Draupnir ring, the magical talisman that the king of the gods Odin had placed on the stake of the wise Baldr, and said, "From this ring," he asserted, "every nine nights eight others of equal value are born."

Aurboða said she did not even want the magical ring, stating, " in my father's gardens gold is in abundance, I certainly do not lack it and never will."

To defeat the woman's obstinacy, the messenger stopped paying compliments and even proposing gifts. He changed his communication strategy, and stated, " If you do not come with me to the realm of the Æsir, and do not accept the flattery of my ruler, I will put a curse on you. You will suffer the worst pains of the underworld, you will live constantly with your eyes turned to the world of the dead. You will lie only with monstrous and foul giants and drink goat piss. You will forget the taste of fresh food and clean air."

The beautiful giantess did not seem particularly shaken; she was certainly afraid of Skírnir's threats, but she knew she was in an advantageous position. At one point Freyr's messenger recoiled, drawing his sword and saying that he would kill her father if she did not be persuaded. The giantess' attention, however, did not focus on the threats but on Freyr's sword. Aurboða was a lover and great connoisseur of the best fighting weapons in existence. She knew the value of the sword unsheathed by the messenger and so she made, she, a proposal to Freyr's servant, stating, " I will go with you, I will marry Freyr, and perhaps in time, I may even love him truly but in return I want his sword." So the somewhat stunned messenger immediately agreed and set off on his steed to Asgard, together with the beautiful giantess. This story taught Freyr that to conquer a woman one should not cover her with gold, but with what she really needs. Aurboða's passion for weapons was the key to the young giantess's heart.

11.8 Baldr's death

It all began when Baldr, also referred to as "Baldr the Good," dreamed of his death. Concerned about the constant nightmares he alerted the Æsir, who immediately assembled a special council. To avert any harmful event against him, the gods decided that they wanted to obtain guarantees for his safety.

Frigg made every living being in the nine realms swear an oath that he would never harm good Baldr. Every element and animal of the earth pledged not to harm Baldr. No blade, no flame, no stone, no poison, no disease, no nothing was to harm young Æsir.

This was what the gods and Frigg had decided. But Loki, god of deceit and cunning loved to stir up strife and especially loved not obeying any kind of order. Loki had never fully appreciated young Baldr, always so good, always liked by everyone, never a controversy with anyone. Loki hated the aura of positivity that hovered when Baldr passed on the street.

At this point, Loki decided to devise a plan to kill Baldr. He took the form of a woman, and pretending to be an ordinary person, he asked Frigg what the gods had decided in council.

Frigg affirmed, "No weapon, no element of nature and no being will be able to harm Baldr, they all swore."

Loki, going into more detail, asked again, "Are you sure all things are sworn to spare Baldr?"

Frigg answered him, "There is a small plant growing east of Valhalla called mistletoe; I thought it was too young to ask for an oath."

Having obtained the information he needed to carry out his plan, Loki left.

He took the mistletoe seedling, weeded it and headed to the Æsir. All the gods were in a circle to pay homage to the oath. Höðr, was alone and outside the circle, since he was blind. Loki caught up with him and asked, " Hool, why don't you throw something at Baldr?"

Baldr replied, "Because I don't see him, and then I don't have anything to throw at him."

Loki said, "Do what others do. Pay homage to Baldr. I will guide you and help you find him. Hit him with this stick."

Höðr took the mistletoe and threw it at Baldr as Loki suggested. Good Baldr tripped over the mistletoe thrown by Hool and fell to the ground, hitting his head hard.

This episode was one of the most dramatic ever to occur in Asgard and shook all the Æsir, no one excluded.

The gods tried, in vain, to revive poor Baldr, but there was nothing more they could do. They looked at each other, tears spilled copiously from the swollen and tired eyes of the gods, and the first thing they thought of was to avenge the poor boy's death.

However, revenge in that place was neither desirable nor applicable; it was a very sacred place for the Asgardians and any impure act including murder, would be detrimental to all the Æsir people.

None of the gods were so lucid as to be able to speak. All were suffering terribly, especially Odin. The father of the gods suffered more than anyone else precisely because he knew how important Baldr was to Asgardian society.

As soon as the gods recovered from the severe trauma, Frigg immediately asked who among the Æsir wanted to gain all his love and benevolence by going after Baldr on the streets of Hel bringing him safely back to Asgard.

Hermóðr the fearless, one of Odin's many sons, volunteered for this venture. He climbed on the back of Sleipnir, Odin's steed, and set out on this venture.

The Æsir took the body of good Baldr and carried it to the sea.

Hringhorni was chosen as the funerary vessel for Baldr. It was the largest vessel of all.

Later Baldr's body was brought to the ship. Baldr's mother and wife on seeing the scene fainted and died as well. Their hearts could not bear such grief. They, too, therefore, were placed on Baldr's funeral ship.

Thor was present and consecrated the funeral pyre with his sacred hammer. Beings of various lineages and descendants participated in this cremation ceremony. Prominent over all were the Asgardians and their ruler Odin, accompanied by Frigg, his Valkyries and ravens. Freyr arrived in the chariot drawn by the pig called "Gullinbursti" or "Slidrugtanni." Even many giants arrived at peace with the Asgardians, just to bid farewell to good Baldr.

Odin threw the golden ring called Draupnir into the stake. This ring had a great peculiarity: every night, eight others of equal size and value were born from the mother ring

Baldr's steed was also brought before the funeral pile.

The story goes that Hermóðr rode on his steed for nine long nights through valleys so dark and deep that he could not see the tip of his nose until he reached a stream; it was the Gjöll River. He galloped over the huge bridge above it. It was covered with a shining golden mantle. Above this magnificent mountain was a virgin called Móðguðr. He asked Hermóðr who she was and where she came from. Once he introduced himself, the fearless warrior asked the virgin if she had seen a man who matched Baldr's description. Móðguðr was greatly astonished that a man with such a likeness would cross the bridge in the direction of Hel. Then she asked him, "Warrior, why are you heading toward Hel?" and he said, "I absolutely must retrieve the man I described to you; I am willing to do anything. Did you see him pass by?"

The virgin replied, "Yes, I saw a man with a rather pink face, looking like a fish out of water. He crossed the Gioll Bridge in the direction of Hel."

Móðguðr, happy to have obtained the information he was seeking, mounted his steed and rode relentlessly toward Hel's gates.

With a huge leap Móðguðr's mighty horse passed all levels of Hel's gateway until it reached the main hall.

He entered and saw Baldr sitting on the highest seat. Hermóðr in the impossibility of reaching him, spent the night there.

The next morning, Hermóðr asked Hel to tell young Baldr that he would not stay a minute longer and would take him home to Asgard, where everyone was apprehensive about him.

The queen of the underworld told the warrior that this was the perfect opportunity to see how fond the people of earth really were of Baldr, stating: " if all the people of the world mourn Baldr's passing, the latter may return with you to Asgard." So, Hermóðr galloped with all his might toward Asgard to tell the Æsir what the queen of the underworld had told him.

Immediately the gods arranged a meeting and decided to send Asgardian emissaries to all nine realms to persuade each living being to mourn for the untimely demise of the young Asgardian so that he could be taken from the realm of the dead by the queen and daughter of Loki, Hel.

And they all did, humans and every other living creature, the earth, the stones, the trees and every other element. Everyone.

When the messengers returned home, having done their work well, they found an old woman on their return journey to Asgard. Her name was Pökk.

They begged her to weep for young Baldr so they could finally take him home. But she affirmed, "I have no eyes to mourn Baldr. What on earth has that young man done for me? I am glad he is going to the house of Hel!" The idea arose among the Asgardian messengers that that person was not just any old woman, but Loki; famous for his deceptions and disguises.

All this sent the Æsir into a rage, who were intent on getting revenge by capturing Loki and taking him to Asgard to judge him. But Loki escaped from Asgard and hid in a mountain. Here, Loki built himself a dwelling with four gates so that he could look in every direction. During the day, Loki mutated into a salmon by hiding in a small river nearby.

In the evening, the God of Deception sat by the fire wondering what punishment the gods would inflict on him.

One day, Loki looking out one of his windows noticed the gods heading toward him. He quickly left the house and headed for the river.

When the Æsir arrived at the house, Kvasir was the first to enter. Kvasir looked around and saw the embers still glowing. That was the sign of a recently lit fire. He realized that Loki was near and that to escape he must have transformed into some being. Looking at the river, Kvasir, who was one of the craftiest and shrewdest Æsirs, immediately realized that Loki was there in the guise of a fish. He spoke to the Æsir about his findings, who treasured them.

At this point in the legend we have been handed down by historians, who translated the Scandinavian transcriptions, two endings: one where Loki is captured and tortured along with his three sons, Fenrir the wolf, the serpent, and Hel, from whom later the legends we already know will arise.

Another ending, however, is that Loki has managed to swim upstream, just as salmon do, and that, by going over waterfalls, he has managed to escape from the clutches of the gods. We like to think that the second ending makes the most sense for a character as cunning and cunning as he is cowardly as the god of deception Loki.

www.ingramcontent.com/pod-product-compliance
Lightning Source LLC
Chambersburg PA
CBHW071451080526
44587CB00014B/2073